# Adam's Big Pot

## Easy meals for your family
### Adam Liaw

hachette
AUSTRALIA

To my grandmother, for who feeding our family has been a life's work

And to my son, who I look forward to cooking for for the rest of my life

# contents

# Introduction

## Why we cook

There will never be enough time in each day to do everything we want to. That's something we all know too well. It's what we *choose* to do with the time we have that is most important.

For me, there is no more worthwhile labour in a kitchen than feeding a family. Choosing dishes, collecting ingredients, and applying time and effort to the task of preparing a family meal gives a result so much more than just a full stomach.

For most of us, a love of food is born around a family dinner table. It definitely was in my case. The dishes we are served by our loved ones as children will, years later, become the dishes we crave as adults. Those dishes shape our palates and also the way we think about food.

It is not just what we eat that is important. Around the family table we share food and we share ideas. Those moments spent in each other's company, away from ringing phones, flashing screens and 24-hour news are, these days, more important than ever.

It's incredible to think how many of the conversations we have with our loved ones take place across a table, and over a plate.

There's nothing wrong with a bit of takeaway, and I'm certainly no stranger to it, but as a new father I would not feel right if I took from my son the privilege I had as a child of experiencing meals full of soul, cooked by my parents and grandparents, and served to me and my brothers and sisters.

As an adult, I still crave my grandma's chicken rice, my mum's lamb chops and my dad's rice, which he would cook in rich chicken stock with pats of melting butter. Even as I think of those dishes now, I recall my happy childhood that was all the richer because of the meals I shared with my family. I'm not sure the same emotions can be linked to the contents of a takeaway container, shovelled down in front of a TV.

To make those family meals and create those memories, sometimes all we need is a little help with our time. A minute saved here and there can take the task of preparing dinner from a tedious chore to a joyful experience and an expression of love.

Make some **Garlic Oil and Garlic Paste (page 23)** and you'll save yourself a few minutes each night when time is at its most precious. Prepare an easy batch of **Chi-Thai Sauce (page 22)** in advance and dishes like **Chicken, Mushrooms and Snow Peas (page 74)** or **Chi-Thai Noodles (page 70)** are just moments away. Best of all, they'll be your dishes – flavours that you created, not ones delivered to your door or borrowed out of a bottle.

A bit of preparation is a great habit, but far and away the best way to save time in the kitchen is to choose dishes that are easy to make. This book is full of those.

In this collection of recipes I've included the dishes I make for my family. Dishes that I don't just find delicious and interesting, but that are also simple enough that I'm not spending more time making the meal than sharing it.

# The shared meal

Particularly in Asian cuisines, a shared meal is often defined by its variety. A range of dishes are served in the middle of the table and shared by those around it. Take a piece of whatever you like then move on to the next.

My grandmother says a well-constructed shared meal should contain an odd number of dishes, with a minimum of three. The same variety that makes a shared Asian meal so appealing can also be intimidating for those new to Asian cooking. If you're baulking at the thought of cooking three, five or even seven different dishes for a simple weeknight dinner, take heart in the fact that you don't have to.

An Asian meal isn't always a banquet spread. There are many exceptional and authentic dishes that are perfect for feeding a family from just one big wok, pan, dish or pot. The bigger the family, the bigger the pot. Most of my favourite dishes from my childhood were made in this way and it is why I have called this cookbook *Adam's Big Pot*. I want to help make preparing family meals easier and give you some new answers for that age-old question: 'What's for dinner?'

A big pot of **Mulligatawny Soup (page 111)**, a big bowl of **Vietnamese Chicken and Mint Salad (page 38)**, a big wok of **Mee Goreng (page 73)**, or a big pan of **Yurinchi (page 159)** are perfect family dinners – simple to prepare and ready to share with a crowd at a moment's notice.

If you still crave the variety of a full table, just add a few sides. Prepare a **Tomato Salad (page 227)**, some **Ajat (page 228)**, or a bowl of **Basic Miso Soup (page 225)** and see the difference they make. A simple side dish or two can have a huge impact on a meal that far outweighs the time taken to prepare them.

# Trying something new

There's a misconception that trying to do something different or new is difficult.

Of course, there are dishes we know like the back of our hands. Old favourites that we have committed to memory and that we could cook with our eyes shut. If those dishes were all that you wanted to cook, you wouldn't be reading this now.

The thing to remember with those family favourites is, they didn't start out that way. Every dish we know began as something we cooked for the first time. It was only after we came to love them that they started to get that little bit easier.

One of the most amazing things about food is that trying something new requires nothing more than the set of skills you already have, but the benefits that come from that are enormous.

You don't need to speak Swahili to make a pot of **Kuku Paka (page 91)**. Even if you've never been to Vietnam you can whip up an authentic **Shaking Beef (page 144)**. There's no university in the world that gives out degrees for **Lamb Vindaloo (page 107)**. But you can easily add them to your family favourites.

I hope somewhere in this book there is a dish or two that you choose to serve to your family. Something that gets asked for again and again, and each time you make it, it becomes a little more your own. Then one day, years from now, when the people you cook for have left and live their lives and come back to visit, you make that meal for them again. And that's what makes them feel like they're home.

Adam

bits &
pieces

½ Chinese cabbage, roughly chopped
¼ cup fish sauce
2 tbsp sake
2 litres water

Place the Chinese cabbage in a large pot and cook over medium heat for 10 minutes, stirring occasionally until the cabbage softens and releases its juices. Add the fish sauce, sake and water and bring to the boil. Simmer for 20 minutes until the cabbage is very soft. Strain the broth and store it in a covered container in the fridge. It will keep for about a week in the fridge, or longer if frozen.

**TIP** / Cabbage Dashi is great as a base for Basic Miso Soup (page 225), White Stew (page 103), or Nikujaga (page 104), and the leftover cooked Chinese cabbage can be added to soups or stews such as the Sumo Stew (page 108). If you ever find your stocks to be lacking in flavour the problem can usually be resolved by adding something salty. Using fish sauce is a great way to add both saltiness and umami to almost any stock. For a vegetarian version, substitute the fish sauce with 1 tbsp salt.

5 sheets nori, torn into pieces
A handful bonito flakes
1 tsp salt flakes
250g unsalted butter, softened

Place the nori and bonito flakes in a food processor or spice grinder and process to a coarse powder.

Mix the nori powder and salt through the softened butter, cover in cling wrap and store in the fridge for up to three months, or longer in the freezer.

**TIP** / Try nori butter brushed on a cooked steak to give it a little extra flavour, or have a go at the Whiting with Nori Butter (page 155), Steak and Asparagus Donburi (page 156), or Nori Butter Roast Chicken (page 179).

# Cabbage dashi

A traditional Japanese ichiban dashi is made with kombu seaweed and dried bonito flakes, but this cabbage version uses ingredients easily found in your local supermarket. Chinese cabbage contains lots of light, umami-rich juices that can be put to good use. Think of this as an all-purpose Asian vegetable stock – it's perfect as a base for soups and braised dishes.

**Makes** / 2 litres
**Prep** / 5 minutes **Cook** / 30 minutes

# Nori butter

Can there be a simpler way of adding flavour than through a compound butter? Nori seaweed sheets, which are commonly used to wrap sushi rolls, are full of nutty flavour. This butter is amazing brushed on grilled scallops, fish, beef, roast chicken, potatoes or anything, really.

**Makes** / 250g
**Prep** / 10 minutes

1 whole free-range chicken (about 1.6kg)
2 tsp salt
About 4 litres water

Rinse the chicken well under running water and remove any visible fat. Rub the salt all over the chicken, including inside the cavity.

Place the chicken breast-down in a large pot. Cover with the water. Bring to a simmer, skimming any scum off the top. This will take around 10–15 minutes. Reduce the heat to very low and simmer for 1 hour uncovered, then turn off the heat, cover the pot and let it stand for a further 30 minutes.

Remove the chicken from the pot and strain the stock. Chill the chicken in the fridge until cool enough to handle, then shred the meat with your fingers, discarding the skin and bones. Keep the shredded chicken meat and stock separately in the fridge. They will each keep for about a week, or longer if frozen.

TIP / Use the shredded chicken in the Vietnamese Chicken and Mint Salad (page 38) or in a Big Red Curry (page 100). The stock is great for Mulligatawny Soup (page 111), Grandma's Tofu (page 69), or Big Pot Noodles (page 95). Or use them both together for some Chinese Chicken and Corn Soup (page 112).

2 tbsp vegetable oil
About 500g raw prawn heads and shells
1 tbsp salt
1½ litres water

Heat the oil in a large saucepan over medium heat and add the prawn pieces and salt. Fry for about 5 minutes, lightly crushing the heads and shells with a wooden spoon and stirring until they change colour to a vibrant orange.

Add the water and bring to the boil. Simmer for 10 minutes, then strain the solids, leaving a flavoursome orange-red stock. The stock will keep in the fridge for about three days, or in the freezer for about three months.

TIP / A good Prawn Stock is the secret to a delicious Tom Yum Soup (page 123), and it's also great in a Big Red Curry (page 100). For something really special, use Prawn Stock to cook the rice for making Omuraisu (page 160). You can use the same method to make a simple fish stock from raw fish bones. Just increase the simmering time to half an hour.

# Whole chicken stock & shredded chicken

This simple recipe is a great Sunday habit. A few minutes of preparation and a bit of time cooking on the stove and you're left with plenty of chicken for salads, sandwiches or any number of other uses throughout the week, as well as a versatile stock.

**Makes** / About 3 litres stock & 4 cups chicken
**Prep** / 5 minutes   **Cook** / 1 hour 15 minutes
**Stand** / 30 minutes

# Prawn stock

So many bits and pieces left over from cooking can be put to excellent use, extracting flavours that might otherwise have gone to waste. Prawn shells are a great example. Instead of consigning them to the bin, just 15 minutes of effort will produce a rich stock that will improve your soups, curries or even stir-fried dishes immeasurably.

**Makes** / 1½ litres
**Cook** / 15 minutes

300g long red chillies (deseeded, if you prefer)
6 cloves garlic
2 cups white vinegar
2 cups sugar
½ cup fish sauce

Roughly chop the chillies and garlic together on a chopping board, or use a food processor.

Bring the vinegar, sugar and fish sauce to the boil in a non-reactive saucepan, stirring to dissolve the sugar. Add the chilli and garlic mix and simmer, uncovered, for about 30 minutes, or until the sauce has thickened. Allow to cool and transfer to a bottle. It will keep in the fridge for around six months.

TIP / Try this with Thai Grilled Chicken (page 169), Barbecued Squid Salad (page 45) or Baked Thai Fish Cakes (page 172). My grandmother always told me that to avoid the residue on your hands burning everything you touch after handling chillies, just wash your hands well with soap, dry them and run them through your hair. It really works!

¼ cup soy sauce
¼ cup fish sauce
½ cup oyster sauce
1 cup dark soy sauce
¼ cup caster sugar
¼ cup Garlic Oil (page 23)
¼ cup Shaoxing wine
1 tbsp cornflour, mixed with 2 tbsp cold water

Combine all the ingredients except the cornflour mixture in a small saucepan over low heat and stir to dissolve the sugar. Bring to a low simmer and slowly add the cornflour mixture, continuing to stir through until the sauce combines and thickens.

Remove from the heat and allow to cool. Transfer to a jar or bottle and store in the fridge until ready to use. It will keep for about six months, refrigerated.

TIP / Try this sauce with any kind of simple stir-fried dish, like Chicken, Mushrooms and Snow Peas (page 74), Chi-Thai Noodles (page 70), or Pork, Green Beans and Lime Leaf (page 78). It makes a great gift as well, so make a big batch and share the love. If your friends are anything like mine, they'll really appreciate it.

# Sweet chilli sauce

A good sweet chilli sauce is a beautiful accompaniment to many Thai dishes. Commercially bottled brands can lack a balance of sweet, sour and savoury flavours, but that's a problem very easily fixed by making your own at home.

**Makes** / 750ml
**Prep** / 10 minutes **Cook** / 35 minutes

# Chi-Thai sauce

During centuries of Chinese migration around Southeast Asia, Chinese dishes were adapted to suit local ingredients and tastes. This multi-purpose 'stir-fry sauce' combines the flavours of China and Thailand and, used sparingly, it enhances the natural flavours of fresh ingredients rather than overwhelming them. The result is a stir-fried dish that tastes of the ingredients chosen rather than just the sauce.

**Makes** / 2½ cups
**Prep** / 5 minutes **Cook** / 5 minutes

2 cups peanut oil
1 cup garlic cloves, peeled

Heat half a cup of the peanut oil in a wide saucepan over medium heat. Add the garlic cloves and brown lightly. Add the remaining oil and heat over low heat (or in a 120°C oven) for 30 minutes. Allow to cool and strain the garlic cloves from the oil.

Mash the garlic cloves to a paste and transfer to a jar, top with a few spoonfuls of the garlic oil. The paste will keep in the fridge for up to two months. Pour the oil into a bottle. This can be kept in the pantry for about two months.

**TIP** / Use the Garlic Oil to make some Chi-Thai Sauce (page 22) or in any stir-fried dish calling for garlic, or combine the oil and paste to make some Garlic Prawns and Broccoli (page 143) or Garlic Miso Chicken (page 140). Peanut oil adds a slightly nutty, toasted flavour to your cooking. It works really well with the garlic, but if you prefer to use another oil, any vegetable oil will do.

4 stalks lemongrass, white part only, roughly chopped
8 cloves garlic, peeled
3 tbsp grated ginger
6 kaffir lime leaves, sliced
2 eschalots, peeled and roughly chopped
4 bird's-eye chillies, or 2 long red chillies for a milder paste
2 tbsp caster sugar
¼ cup lime juice
¼ cup fish sauce

Combine the solid ingredients in a mortar and pound to a fine paste, then mix through the liquid ingredients. Alternatively, blend all the ingredients to a smooth paste in a blender, adding extra water to ensure they blend well.

Transfer the paste to an airtight jar if using within two to three days, otherwise freeze tablespoons of the paste in an ice cube tray until solid, then transfer to a freezer bag for up to six months.

**TIP** / If you make a double batch of this paste, it will be plenty to make the Tom Yum Fried Rice (page 86), Tom Yum Soup (page 123) and Baked Tom Yum and Coconut Snapper (page 192). You can even freeze the paste in the correct portions for those recipes.

# Garlic oil & garlic paste

Saving time while cooking a family meal can often just be a matter of shaving off a minute here and there with some good preparation. This garlic oil is simple to make and does double duty: the oil can be used for almost any recipe that starts with frying garlic, and the paste can substitute for chopped garlic.

# Tom yum paste

Tom yum is easy to make fresh, but you can't beat the convenience of a ready-to-go paste. Commercial pastes are fried in oil to preserve them, which takes away some of the light freshness. I prefer to make my own paste and freeze it in portions, which can be added to a stock for an instant soup.

**Makes** / About 2 cups oil & ½ cup garlic paste
**Prep** / 5 minutes **Cook** / 30 minutes

**Makes** / 1 cup
**Prep** / 15 minutes

- 50g dried large red chillies, seeds and stalks removed
- 10 large red chillies, seeds and stalks removed and roughly chopped
- 10 coriander roots, leaves, stems and roots roughly chopped
- 2 small red onions, peeled and roughly chopped
- 3 stalks lemongrass, white part only, roughly chopped
- 6 kaffir lime leaves, roughly sliced
- 10 cloves garlic, peeled
- 3 tbsp grated ginger
- 2 tbsp ground coriander
- 1 tsp ground black pepper
- 2 tsp salt
- ½ cup fish sauce

Soak the dried chillies in hot water for half an hour then drain well. Combine the soaked dried chillies with the remaining ingredients in a blender or food processor and blend or process to a smooth paste. You can add a little extra fish sauce to your blender to get it to catch the paste if you need to. The curry paste will keep in the fridge for about two weeks, but I prefer to freeze it in ½-cup batches immediately to keep it fresh.

**TIP** / Use this paste for a Big Red Curry (page 100), Baked Thai Fish Cakes (page 172), or even as a rub for roast beef or chicken. If you can't find dried large red chillies you can use smaller dried chillies, but the paste will be spicier.

# Easy red curry paste

Making your own curry paste when there are so many good commercial pastes available might seem like extra work, but it's worth the effort for the fresh and individual flavour you can produce. Enlist some help from a friend and make a big batch to share between you. You will definitely use it all.

**Makes** / 2 cups
**Prep** / 45 minutes

½ cup lime juice or lemon juice (or a mixture of juice and rice vinegar)
¼ cup caster sugar
About ½ cup fish sauce
2 bird's-eye chillies, finely chopped (seeds removed if you wish)
3 cloves garlic, peeled and crushed
¾ cup water, to dilute

Mix together the juice, vinegar (if using) and sugar and stir to dissolve the sugar. Taste the mixture. It should taste pleasant and have a good balance of sweet and sour, like a well-made lemonade. (Vinegars and fruit have varying levels of acidity so you may need to add a little more sugar).

Add the fish sauce gradually, tasting as you go until the mixture changes noticeably from sweet to quite savoury. Add a little more fish sauce then stir through the chillies and garlic. Allow to stand for at least 10 minutes before using. If using immediately, dilute the Nuoc Cham with the water and serve, otherwise store it in the fridge undiluted. It will keep for about one month in the fridge.

TIP / If you have a mortar and pestle you can use it to get even more flavour into this sauce by pounding the chilli and garlic together first, then making the Nuoc Cham in the mortar.

3 cups raw white rice
About 5 cups water (see Method)

Wash the rice well by covering the grains in the pot with water and stirring with your hand. Pour off the starchy, cloudy water, being careful not to lose any grains. Repeat the process three or four times until the water runs clear.

Place the washed rice in a medium saucepan and add cold water to about 3cm above the top of the rice. Bring the rice and water to the boil over high heat and boil, uncovered, until the water level drops to the top of the rice. Small holes in the surface of the rice will appear where steam escapes. Reduce heat to very low and cover the saucepan with a lid. Cook, covered, for 12–15 minutes, then turn off the heat and let the rice stand for a further 5 minutes without removing the lid. Alternatively, microwave the rice in a microwave-safe dish for 15–18 minutes then stand for 5 minutes. Uncover and with a cutting motion of a spatula, fluff the rice grains.

TIP / A simple way to measure the water level is to touch the top of your middle finger to the surface of the rice. The water should reach the line of your first knuckle. At home I use three varieties of rice regularly. Short-grain Japanese koshihikari rice for East Asian food; jasmine rice for Southeast Asian food; and short-grain brown rice for something different. Try a few varieties to find which you like best.

# Nuoc cham

This Vietnamese sauce is extremely versatile. Use it over grilled meats, as a dressing for salads or as a dipping sauce in any number of Asian dishes. The key is to balance the sweet, sour and savoury elements, and using this method you'll never fail.

**Makes** / 1 cup (undiluted)
**Prep** / 10 minutes  **Stand** / 10 minutes

# Steamed rice

A bit of confusion surrounds the term 'steamed rice'. It isn't done in a steamer, nor is it boiled and drained like pasta. Instead, it's cooked in water so that the grains absorb the liquid and steam in their own moisture over low heat. Most Asian families use a rice cooker, but making steamed rice on the stovetop or in the microwave is very easy.

**Makes** / 4½ cups
**Prep** / 5 minutes  **Cook** / 20 minutes
**Stand** / 5 minutes

½ cup crushed garlic, or Garlic Paste (page 23)

¼ cup grated ginger

3 tbsp paprika

1 tbsp chilli powder

3 tbsp ground turmeric

3 tsp ground cumin

2 tsp ground coriander

2 tsp garam masala

1 tsp ground cardamom

2 tbsp tomato paste

2 tbsp soft brown sugar

2 tbsp white vinegar

2 tsp salt

Mix together all the ingredients to create a smooth paste. Keep in an airtight container in the fridge for up to one month, or make a double quantity and freeze portions of the mixture in an ice cube tray. Once frozen, you can transfer the cubes to a freezer bag and keep them for up to a year.

TIP / This paste is the starting point for a great homemade Tandoori Chicken (page 191) or Butter Chicken (page 129). It's also great on lamb chops for the barbecue. If you're freezing the paste, first line the ice cube tray with cling wrap to avoid the turmeric staining the plastic.

# Tandoori paste

This simple paste just needs to be mixed with fresh yoghurt to make an easy marinade for chicken, fish, lamb or even vegetables. It keeps well in the fridge and can easily be frozen. Don't be afraid to change the quantities of the spices to make it your own.

**Makes** / About 1 cup
**Prep** / 5 minutes

big
bowl

2 cloves garlic, peeled

2 bird's-eye chillies

1 tbsp dried shrimp, soaked in hot
    water for 20 minutes (optional)

50ml lime juice

2 tsp palm sugar or caster sugar

1 tbsp fish sauce

1 continental cucumber, peeled,
    deseeded and cut into matchsticks

1 small carrot, peeled and cut into
    matchsticks

1 cup green beans or snake beans,
    trimmed and cut into 5cm lengths

10 cherry tomatoes, halved

¼ cup crushed roasted peanuts

In a large mortar place the garlic, chillies and dried shrimp (if using) and pound to a rough paste. Add the lime juice and sugar and continue to pound until the sugar dissolves. Taste the mixture and adjust the sweetness if necessary with more sugar or lime juice – it should be slightly sweet, like lemonade. Then add the fish sauce a little at a time until the dressing tastes quite savoury.

Add the cucumber, carrot, beans and tomatoes and gently pound them to bruise them and release their juices. Stir the peanuts through and serve.

TIP / For a larger meal, stir through some crab meat, cooked prawns or Shredded Chicken (page 18).

# Carrot & cucumber som tam

Som tam is best known outside Thailand as 'green papaya salad', but it is actually less about the papaya and more about the process. Lightly pounding vegetables releases their juices which mix into a fresh, flavourful dressing. This carrot and cucumber version is light and delicious, and you don't need to track down green papayas, which aren't always available.

**Serves** / 2 (or more as part of a shared meal)

**Soak** / 20 minutes  **Prep** / 10 minutes

1kg fresh or frozen udon noodles
4 Steamed Eggs (page 228), Tea Eggs
    (page 220), or hard-boiled eggs,
    halved
2 cups finely shredded cabbage
1 Lebanese cucumber, peeled
    in intervals and cut into thin
    matchsticks
1 cup picked coriander leaves
3 spring onions, trimmed and
    finely sliced
½ cup crushed roasted peanuts

**DRESSING**
½ cup peanut oil
6 cloves garlic, peeled and roughly
    chopped
3 dried red chillies, sliced, or
    1 tsp chilli flakes
1 tsp caster sugar
4 tbsp fish sauce
½ cup lemon juice

Cook the noodles according to the packet instructions and drain well. Transfer to a large platter and top with halved eggs and piles of the cabbage, cucumber, coriander, spring onions and crushed peanuts.

To make the dressing, heat the peanut oil in a small frypan over medium heat and fry the garlic until it begins to brown. Add the chilli and continue to fry until the garlic and chilli are well toasted. Turn off the heat and add the sugar, fish sauce and lemon juice. Stir well and pour the hot dressing straight over the noodles and other ingredients. Toss to combine and serve.

TIP / Try this with some cooked rice vermicelli noodles in place of the udon. If you want to add some meat just throw in a bit of Shredded Chicken (page 18) or even some Shaking Beef (page 144).

# Udon with friends

This is the perfect summer lunch or light dinner, and it can be served at any temperature, from chilled through to warm. This simple shared noodle dish collects together some udon noodles with a few of their favourite companions.

**Serves** / 4
**Prep** / 20 minutes  **Cook** / 10 minutes

¼ cup desiccated coconut

12 large raw prawns, peeled and deveined

1 pink grapefruit

2 small Lebanese cucumbers, peeled in intervals and thinly sliced

1 cup picked coriander leaves

½ cup crushed roasted peanuts

¼ cup fried shallots

Sliced chillies, to serve (optional)

**DRESSING**

3 tbsp undiluted Nuoc Cham (page 27)

*OR*

50ml lime juice

2 tsp caster sugar

2 tbsp fish sauce

1 clove garlic, crushed

In a dry frypan, toast the coconut over medium heat, tossing frequently until the coconut is light brown. Set aside to cool.

Slice the prawns completely in half lengthways. Bring a small pot of water to the boil and poach the prawns for about 2 minutes until they are just cooked through and curled into spirals. Peel the grapefruit and break the flesh into bite-sized segments, discarding as much of the white pith as possible.

If making the dressing, mix the ingredients together and stir to dissolve the sugar.

Place the cooked prawns, grapefruit, cucumber, toasted coconut, coriander leaves and peanuts in a bowl with the Nuoc Cham or dressing and toss well. Serve scattered with fried shallots and sliced chillies, if using.

TIP / Fried shallots are available in the Asian section of many supermarkets. Splitting the prawns lengthways allows them to curl into spirals when cooking to give the salad texture and volume. It's also a great technique when using prawns in fried rice or noodle dishes.

# Prawn & grapefruit salad

This salad is a lovely balance of the freshness of grapefruit and the rich, toasted flavour of coconut, shallots and nuts. In Thailand this is usually made from pomelo, but grapefruit works just as well. It's a great light meal for summer.

**Serves** / 4
**Prep** / 15 minutes  **Cook** / 10 minutes

½ head cabbage, finely shredded

½ red onion, peeled and very
    finely sliced

2 cups loosely packed mint,
    roughly torn

1 carrot, peeled and cut into very
    thin matchsticks

2 cups Shredded Chicken (page 18)

¼ cup fried shallots

¼ cup crushed roasted peanuts

**DRESSING**

½ cup undiluted Nuoc Cham (page 27)

*OR*

100ml lemon juice

1 tbsp caster sugar

2 tbsp fish sauce

1 bird's-eye chilli, seeds removed
    and finely sliced

1 clove garlic, minced

If making the dressing, mix the ingredients together and allow to stand for a few minutes.

In a large bowl, combine all the ingredients for the salad except the shallots and peanuts and toss to combine. Pour over the Nuoc Cham or dressing and toss again to coat. Transfer to a serving plate or bowl and scatter with the shallots and peanuts.

**TIP** / To shred the cabbage and onion I use a mandoline slicer – it's done in seconds, but you really have to watch your fingers!

# Vietnamese chicken & mint salad

**Goi ga** / Vietnamese cuisine really does have it sorted out. You can create vibrant, layered flavours in minutes, and from a minimal number of ingredients. Even if you've never made Vietnamese food before, give this salad a try. It's light, fresh and flavourful, and it'll become a regular dinner in your household, just as it has in mine.

**Serves** / 4
**Prep** / 20 minutes

1 rump steak (about 500g)
   or 2 sirloin steaks (about 250g each)
Salt, to season
1 tsp vegetable oil
3 Roma tomatoes, cut into wedges
1 Lebanese cucumber, split in half
   lengthways, seeds removed
   and sliced
1 red onion, peeled and very
   thinly sliced
1 cup picked coriander leaves
Green oak lettuce leaves, to serve

**ROASTED RICE POWDER**
1 tsp uncooked jasmine rice

**DRESSING**
50ml lime juice
2 tsp caster sugar
2 tbsp fish sauce
1 clove garlic, peeled and crushed
2 red bird's-eye chillies, thinly sliced
   (or to taste)
1 tsp roasted rice powder (optional)
   (see above)
1 tsp grated ginger
1 spring onion, trimmed and
   finely sliced

Season the steak well with salt and barbecue or pan-fry with a little oil in a heavy frypan over high heat until well browned and cooked to your liking. (Medium rare is best for this dish). Rest for 5 minutes in a warm, draught-free place then slice thinly.

If making the roasted rice powder, toast the rice in a dry frypan over medium heat until it turns opaque and begins to brown. Grind in a mortar and pestle to a coarse powder.

For the dressing, mix all the ingredients together. Toss the sliced steak, tomato, cucumber, onion and coriander leaves with the dressing and any collected juices after slicing the steak.

Serve the beef salad on the lettuce leaves together with any collected juices and dressing.

**TIP** / Roasted rice powder is a really important element in a lot of Thai dishes as it gives texture to thin dressings and sauces and helps to stick them to other ingredients. In Thailand glutinous rice is commonly used to make rice powder but any white or brown rice works well. If you have some undiluted Nuoc Cham (page 27) on hand you can use 3 tbsp of it to replace the lime juice, caster sugar, fish sauce, garlic and ginger in this dressing.

# Thai beef salad

**Yam neua** / It's easy to see why the simple Thai beef salad is such a popular dish both in Australia and in Thailand – it's fast to make and absolutely delicious. It is also great for a barbecue because the dressing and other ingredients can be prepared in advance, and the steak is simply sliced and tossed through after grilling.

**Serves** / 4
**Prep** / 20 minutes **Cook** / 10 minutes

3 good-quality tuna steaks (about 200g each)
1 tsp peanut oil
1 cup cherry tomatoes, halved
1 red onion, peeled, halved and very thinly sliced
1 Lebanese cucumber, peeled in intervals and very thinly sliced
4 red radishes, trimmed and very thinly sliced
100g mixed baby salad greens
2 tbsp lemon juice
1 sheet nori, toasted and crumbled (see Tip)
1 tsp mixed black and white sesame seeds, toasted (see Tip)

**DRESSING**
2 tbsp mirin
1 tbsp sake
¼ cup soy sauce
A pinch of caster sugar
1 tsp grated ginger

To make the dressing, combine the mirin and sake in a small saucepan and bring to the boil, then remove from the heat and transfer to a bowl. Add the soy sauce, sugar and grated ginger. Mix well and set aside.

If the tuna steaks are very big, halve them along the grain. Heat the peanut oil in a heavy frypan until very hot and sear the tuna for about 20 seconds on each side. The tuna should still be quite raw in the centre. Transfer the tuna to a press-seal bag and pour over a tablespoon of the dressing. Refrigerate for at least 10 minutes. Slice the tuna across the grain into thin slices.

Toss together the tomatoes, onion, cucumber, radish and salad greens. Place on a plate with slices of tuna.

Mix the remaining dressing with the lemon juice and pour over the tuna and salad. Scatter with the crumbled nori and sesame seeds.

TIP / To toast nori, hold a sheet with tongs and wave it over an open gas flame for just a few seconds until it becomes brittle. To toast black sesame seeds, mix them with a few white sesame seeds. When the white seeds turn golden, the black ones will be toasted, too.

# Tuna tataki salad

This really is one of the freshest, lightest salads you'll ever eat. It uses barely any oil and needs almost no cooking, but it has lots of flavour and won't make you feel like you've skipped a meal.

**Serves** / 4
**Prep** / 20 minutes **Refrigerate** / 10 minutes **Cook** / 5 minutes

500g cleaned squid tubes
1 tbsp vegetable oil
2 tbsp Sweet Chilli Sauce (page 22)
 or bottled sweet chilli sauce
1 tbsp fish sauce
2 celery stalks, strings removed and
 very thinly sliced, leaves reserved
1 red onion, peeled and finely sliced
1 kaffir lime leaf, central vein removed
 and leaf very finely sliced
12 cherry tomatoes, halved
½ cup mint leaves, torn
½ cup Thai basil leaves, torn

**DRESSING**
25ml lime juice
1 tsp caster sugar
1 tbsp fish sauce
½ tsp grated ginger

*OR*
2 tbsp undiluted Nuoc Cham (page 27)
½ tsp grated ginger

Cut down one side of each squid tube and open them all out flat. Score the squid lightly in a cross-hatch pattern and cut into large triangles. Mix the squid together with the oil, Sweet Chilli Sauce and fish sauce and set aside to marinate for 5 minutes.

Stir the dressing ingredients together until the sugar is dissolved. If using Nuoc Cham as the dressing, mix in the grated ginger. In a separate bowl, combine the celery, onion, kaffir lime leaf, cherry tomatoes, herbs and a few celery leaves and toss through the dressing.

Grill the squid on a very hot barbecue hotplate or in a heavy frypan over high heat for about 2 minutes, tossing with tongs until the squid is just opaque and the outside is caramelised. Toss the squid through the dressed salad and serve.

**TIP** / Try this with grilled and sliced beef for an interesting variation on a Thai beef salad. You can also substitute the squid for chicken thigh fillets. The chicken will need to be grilled for a few minutes longer to ensure it's cooked through.

# Barbecued squid salad

The combination of caramelised squid, sweet basil and sharp celery really makes this salad. If you want to start working more seafood into your family meals, this is a simple, economical and delicious way to start. It can be done on a barbecue or in a heavy frypan with equal success.

**Serves** / 4
**Prep** / 15 minutes  **Cook** / 10 minutes

1 long red chilli

4 cloves garlic, peeled

½ cup vegetable oil

2 eggplants, halved and thinly sliced on an angle

2 tbsp soy sauce

2 tbsp fish sauce (or additional soy sauce)

1 tbsp caster sugar

½ cup water

½ cup picked coriander leaves (optional)

150g mixed salad greens

2 Lebanese cucumbers, peeled in intervals, halved and thinly sliced diagonally

4 spring onions, trimmed and finely shredded

**BLACK VINEGAR DRESSING**

3 tbsp black vinegar

1 tbsp caster sugar

1 tbsp sesame oil

1 tsp fish sauce

1 tsp oyster sauce

Roughly chop the chilli and garlic together on a board. Heat the oil in a wok or large frypan over medium heat and fry the chilli and garlic until fragrant and starting to brown. Remove the solids from the wok and set aside but keep the oil hot.

Add the eggplant in batches and toss to coat in the oil. Fry each batch over very high heat until the eggplant has soaked up all the oil, then remove from the pan and set aside. When the last batch is cooked, return all the eggplant to the wok and toss through the soy sauce, fish sauce and caster sugar. Add the water a splash at a time while tossing the wok until the eggplant is soft. Toss through the reserved chilli and garlic, and the coriander (if using).

To make the dressing, stir together all the ingredients until the sugar is dissolved. Combine the salad greens, cucumber and spring onion in a large bowl, then toss through the dressing. Scatter the warm eggplant over the greens and serve.

TIP / If you have any leftover Pork and Eggplant (page 85), just dress some herbs and salad greens with the black vinegar dressing and put the leftovers on top to turn them into a simple salad.

# Chilli, garlic & eggplant salad

The spicy garlic flavour of the eggplant in this hearty vegetarian dish makes for a salad that's just as good in colder weather as it is when it's warm. If you don't have any black vinegar for the dressing, just use rice vinegar instead.

**Serves** / 4
**Prep** / 25 minutes **Cook** / 15 minutes

1 cup uncooked quinoa

1 tbsp vegetable oil

3 salmon fillets (about 220g each), pinboned and skin removed

Salt flakes, to season

200g baby spinach (about 6 cups)

4 red radishes, trimmed and very thinly sliced

1 red onion, peeled and very thinly sliced

1 large orange, peeled and cut into segments, discarding any white pith

2 tbsp mixed black and white sesame seeds, toasted

## SESAME DRESSING

1 cup natural yoghurt

2 tbsp tahini

2 tsp sesame oil

1 tbsp soy sauce

1 tbsp rice vinegar

2 tsp honey

1 tsp salt flakes

To cook the quinoa, first wash the uncooked grains in a fine sieve under running water for a few seconds. Transfer to a small saucepan and add 2 cups cold water. Bring to a rolling boil over medium heat then cover the saucepan and reduce the heat to very low. Simmer for 12 minutes then turn off the heat and leave, covered, for a further 5 minutes. Fluff the grains with a spatula and allow to cool, uncovered, until you can no longer see steam escaping from the pot, then cover the pot again and allow to cool to room temperature.

For the dressing, mix all the ingredients together.

Heat the vegetable oil in a large frypan over medium heat. Season the salmon fillets well with salt and fry for about 2½ minutes on each side, or until crisp on the outside and just cooked in the centre. Transfer the salmon to some paper towel to cool slightly (see Tip).

In a large bowl, combine the cooked quinoa, spinach, radish, onion, orange and dressing and toss well to coat. Break the salmon apart into large chunks and gently toss through the salad. Transfer to a serving plate and scatter with the sesame seeds.

TIP / If the salmon fillets are very thick at one end and very thin at the other, separate the thick and thin ends and pan-fry the thin end separately for about 1 minute each side. The thick part can be cooked as per the method.

# Sesame salmon salad

Quick, simple, delicious and light, this is one of our household's favourite midweek meals. The creamy sesame dressing gets additional nuttiness from sesame oil, while the orange and honey provide a bit of sweetness.

**Serves** / 6

**Prep** / 20 minutes  **Cook** / 5 minutes

1 tbsp salt
1 tsp sugar
½ small head cabbage
12 green beans, trimmed
2 cups raw bean sprouts, washed
1 Lebanese cucumber, sliced into
    rounds
2 ripe tomatoes, cut into wedges
4 Steamed Eggs (page 228) or
    hard-boiled eggs, halved
1 block (300g) fried tofu, cut into
    large cubes (optional)
Prawn crackers, to serve (optional)
2 tbsp fried shallots (optional)

## PEANUT SAUCE
2 bird's-eye chillies
2 tbsp palm sugar or brown sugar
½ tsp salt
1 cup unsalted roasted peanuts
3 tbsp fish sauce
1 tbsp lime juice
2 tbsp tamarind paste dissolved in
    1 cup hot water

To make the peanut sauce, grind the chillies in a mortar and pestle with the sugar and salt, then add the peanuts and grind to a coarse paste. Add the fish sauce and lime juice and dilute to a thin dressing by gradually adding the tamarind liquid. Adjust to taste with a little sugar and salt if needed, and set aside.

Bring a large pot of water to the boil and add the salt and sugar. Boil the cabbage for 5 minutes or until just tender, and drain very well. Blanch the beans and bean sprouts separately for 30 seconds each, returning the water to the boil between blanching each vegetable.

Arrange the blanched cabbage, beans and bean sprouts on a plate with the cucumber and tomatoes, as well as the halved eggs and tofu cubes (if using).

Cook the prawn crackers (if using) according to the manufacturer's directions.

Serve the vegetables with the peanut sauce and scattered with the fried shallots.

TIP / The fresh peanut sauce served with this salad can be used for grilled chicken as a lighter alternative to satay sauce that doesn't contain coconut milk.

# Gado gado

This Indonesian salad is simply a mix of blanched and raw vegetables with a light peanut sauce. You can use whatever vegetables you like. Tofu or Shredded Chicken (page 18) also work well, as does a little fresh pineapple.

**Serves** / 4
**Prep** / 20 minutes  **Cook** / 10 minutes

2 tbsp uncooked white or brown rice
1 tsp chilli powder, or to taste
1 tsp chilli flakes, or to taste
1kg chicken mince
½ cup fish sauce
2 tsp caster sugar
½ cup lime juice
1 red onion, peeled, halved and very
    thinly sliced
3 spring onions, trimmed and finely
    chopped
1 cup mint, loosely packed
2 cups coriander, loosely packed
Leaves of 1 baby cos lettuce, to serve
2 Lebanese cucumbers, peeled in
    intervals and thinly sliced, to serve
2 cups green beans, trimmed, to serve
Sliced bird's-eye chillies, to serve

Place the uncooked rice in a dry frypan and heat over medium heat, tossing occasionally for about 2 minutes until white rice begins to turn chalky white and light brown around the edges. If using brown rice, it will begin to brown and smell nutty and toasted. Add the chilli powder and flakes and toss in the pan for a further 30 seconds until the chilli is fragrant. Transfer the rice and chilli to a mortar and pestle and grind to a coarse powder.

Place the chicken in a large frypan over high heat together with ½ cup water and cook, breaking up and stirring regularly, for about 8 minutes until the chicken is cooked through and the liquid is evaporated. Transfer to a large bowl and pour over the fish sauce and caster sugar and stir through. Allow the chicken to cool until it stops steaming and add the lime juice, red onion, spring onion, mint, coriander and the rice and chilli powder mixture. Toss to coat well and serve with the raw vegetables on the side.

**TIP** / This dish is usually made with Thai roasted chilli powder, but it isn't easy to come by outside Thailand. Toasting a mix of ordinary chilli flakes and chilli powder with the roasted rice is a really good substitute.

# Chicken larb

The secret to a good Thai larb is the roasted rice powder, which adds texture and also thickens the dressings, helping them to stick to the chicken. Served with some raw vegetables, it makes for a great light dinner. You could also try this with pork, beef or turkey mince.

**Serves** / 4–6
**Prep** / 15 minutes  **Cook** / 10 minutes

1 large can (425g) tuna in springwater
1 brown or white onion, peeled, halved
     and thinly sliced
1 cup Japanese mayonnaise
1 cup unsweetened Greek-style
     yoghurt
2 tbsp lemon juice plus extra, to taste
4 cobs of corn, kernels stripped
Salt and pepper, to season
½ head red cabbage, very finely
     shredded
1 carrot, cut into very thin matchsticks
2 tbsp finely chopped chives, to serve
Freshly ground black pepper, to serve
1 avocado, quartered lengthways,
     to serve
Lemon wedges, to serve

Drain the tuna and mix with the onion, mayonnaise, yoghurt and lemon juice. Stir through the raw corn kernels. Season with salt and pepper to taste and set aside until ready to use.

Mix together the cabbage and carrot, arrange them in a bowl or on a plate and season with a bit of salt, pepper and extra lemon juice. Top the cabbage with a generous scoop of the tuna mixture.

Scatter with the chives and black pepper and add a thick wedge of avocado. Serve with lemon wedges.

**TIP** / The tuna and corn mixture also makes a great sandwich filling.

# Tuna, corn & avocado salad

The tuna in this salad does double duty as both the main ingredient in the salad and as a dressing. With the flavourful tuna on top, you don't need anything more than a bit of lemon juice, salt and pepper for the vegetables. I like to serve a big piece of avocado on the side, just so I can dig into it whenever I feel like it.

**Serves** / 4
**Prep** / 20 minutes

big
wok

500g pork belly, skin off and deboned
1 tbsp peanut oil
2 cloves garlic, peeled
1cm ginger, thinly sliced
2 tbsp chilli bean sauce
2 tbsp hoisin sauce
1 small green capsicum, deseeded
    and cut into 5cm strips
4 spring onions, trimmed and sliced
    into 5cm lengths
¼ head cabbage, cut into large pieces
1 tbsp light soy sauce
2 tbsp Shaoxing wine
½ tsp salt flakes
Steamed rice, to serve

Place the pork in a large saucepan and cover with cold water. Bring the water to the boil over high heat, then reduce the heat, cover the pot and simmer for 30 minutes. Remove the pork from the liquid and rest it until it is cool enough to handle.

Cut the pork into 5cm-wide strips, then slice each strip into ½cm-wide pieces.

Heat a wok until smoking and add the peanut oil. Bruise the garlic and ginger, leaving them whole. Fry them in the oil until lightly browned then remove them from the wok. Add half the pork pieces and fry them, tossing occasionally until the fat renders and the edges of the pork start to brown and crisp. Remove the first batch from the wok and repeat the process for the remaining pork.

Pour off all but 3 tbsp of oil and return the fried pork to the wok together with the garlic and ginger. Add the chilli bean sauce and hoisin sauce and toss the pork until well coated and the sauces are fragrant. Add the capsicum, spring onions and cabbage together with the soy sauce, Shaoxing wine and salt and toss everything to combine. Continue to toss for a further 5 minutes until the vegetables soften slightly.

Allow to rest for a few minutes before serving. Remove the ginger and garlic cloves and serve with rice.

TIP / Chilli bean sauce (toban djan, or sometimes called chilli bean paste) is a popular Sichuanese paste made from chillies and broad beans. It's available in the Asian section of many supermarkets and from Asian grocers. You can substitute gochujang, a Korean chilli and soy bean paste available from Asian grocers.

# Cook-again pork

**Huí guō ròu** / The Chinese name for this Sichuanese dish translates to 'cook-again pork', referring to the boiling then stir-frying that produces crisp but tender pork. But I like to think of it as having another meaning. Cook this dish once and after you've fallen in love with it, you're sure to cook it again.

**Serves** / 4
**Prep** / 15 minutes  **Cook** / 40 minutes

600g chicken thigh fillets

4 tbsp Chi-Thai sauce (page 22)
or 4 tbsp oyster sauce

3 tbsp Garlic Oil (page 23) or 3 cloves
garlic, peeled, chopped and fried in
3 tbsp vegetable oil

1 red capsicum, deseeded and cut into
5cm x 2cm pieces

6 spring onions, trimmed and cut into
5cm lengths

2 bird's-eye chillies, halved lengthways
(optional)

¾ cup roasted unsalted cashew nuts

1 tbsp cornflour, mixed with 2 tbsp
cold water

Steamed rice, to serve

Slice the chicken thigh fillets into thin strips. Mix with 2 tbsp of the Chi-Thai sauce or oyster sauce and set aside for 10 minutes to marinate.

Heat a wok over high heat and add the Garlic Oil. Add the chicken and toss in the wok until browned. You may need to do this in batches depending on the size of your wok and the size of your flame. Add the capsicum, spring onion, bird's-eye chillies (if using) and remaining 2 tbsp of Chi-Thai or oyster sauce and toss for about 2 minutes, or until the vegetables are softened. Scatter over the cashew nuts and drizzle over the cornflour mixture slowly, tossing until the sauce is thickened. Transfer to a plate and allow to rest for about a minute. Serve with steamed rice.

TIP / For a variation with an Australian flavour, try this with a handful of toasted macadamia nuts instead of cashews.

# Chicken &
# cashew nuts

This dish exists both in Chinese and Thai cooking, having been brought to Thailand as a result of Chinese migration. The two versions are quite different, from the way the ingredients are cut to the method of adding the sauce. This version combines both styles for an easy family meal.

**Serves** / 4
**Prep** / 10 minutes  **Marinate** / 10 minutes  **Cook** / 10 minutes

'The dishes we are served by
our loved ones as children will,
years later, become the dishes
we crave as adults.'

- 600g pork belly, skin and bone removed, thinly sliced
- 1 tbsp vegetable oil
- 2 tbsp gochujang (Korean chilli bean paste)
- 2 tbsp mirin
- 2 tbsp soy sauce
- 2 cups kimchi
- 180g enoki mushrooms, trimmed
- 5 spring onions, trimmed and sliced into 5cm lengths, light green parts finely sliced
- Steamed rice, to serve

Cut the pork belly into 5cm lengths. Heat the oil in a wok over high heat and fry the pork pieces until lightly browned. Add the gochujang, mirin and soy sauce and toss until the pork is coated. Add the kimchi, mushrooms and spring onion lengths and stir-fry until the mushrooms and onions are softened and the kimchi is fragrant.

Scatter with the finely sliced spring onions and serve with steamed short-grain rice.

TIP / Kimchi is the general term for Korean fermented pickled vegetables. There are many different varieties, and as a group kimchi are considered the national food of Korea. This dish is made with the most common variety, a spicy red version made from Chinese cabbage, often with some radish and spring onion included. It is readily available from Asian grocery stores.

# Pork & kimchi

Kimchi is one of those great ingredients that can add a huge amount of flavour without a lot of effort. It's fermented, and the strong umami flavour in good kimchi is created naturally. You can see why it's such a big part of Korean cuisine, and why it's winning fans all over the world.

**Serves** / 4
**Prep** / 10 minutes  **Cook** / 10 minutes

About 2 litres vegetable oil, for deep-frying

500g squid tubes, cleaned

3 tbsp rice flour or cornflour

2 cloves garlic, peeled and roughly chopped

1 bird's-eye chilli, sliced

2 spring onions, trimmed and sliced

1 tsp salt flakes

¼ tsp freshly ground black pepper

Coriander leaves and lemon wedges, to serve

Heat the oil to 200°C in a wok or large saucepan. Cut down one side of the squid tubes and open them flat. Lightly score the surface in a cross-hatch pattern, cut into bite-sized triangles and toss in the flour. Shake off any excess flour and deep-fry the squid in batches for about a minute per batch, or until just cooked and lightly golden. Drain well.

Remove the oil, leaving about a tablespoon in the wok. Heat the wok over medium heat and add the garlic, chilli and spring onion. Toss in the wok for about a minute, or until the ingredients are lightly browned. Add the squid and toss constantly, scattering with the salt and pepper.

Remove the squid from the wok, scatter with coriander leaves and serve with lemon wedges.

TIP / You can use the same mix of salt, pepper, garlic, chilli and spring onion to season fried chicken prepared as for Yurinchi (page 159), or prawns dusted with cornflour and shallow-fried.

# Salt & pepper squid

You could argue that salt and pepper squid is Australia's national dish. It's universally loved and you can buy it in just about any pub, Vietnamese, Thai or Chinese restaurant, or Italian café around the country. On top of that, it's not commonly found in any other country. It is a truly homegrown favourite.

**Serves** / 4
**Prep** / 10 minutes  **Cook** / 5 minutes

2 blocks (600g) soft or silken tofu
2 tbsp Garlic Oil (page 23) or 2 cloves
    garlic, peeled, chopped and fried in
    2 tbsp peanut oil
1 tbsp sesame oil
1 tsp chilli oil (or extra sesame oil if
    you prefer it milder)
500g pork or beef mince
3 tbsp chilli bean sauce
2 tbsp salted black beans, roughly
    crushed, or 2 tbsp black bean sauce
2 tbsp oyster sauce
1 tsp grated ginger
3 tbsp Shaoxing wine
2 tbsp caster sugar
1 tsp Sichuan peppercorns, lightly
    ground
500ml Whole Chicken Stock (page 18)
    or Cabbage Dashi (page 17)
1 tbsp cornflour, mixed with 2 tbsp
    cold water
4 spring onions, trimmed and finely
    chopped
Steamed rice, to serve

Prepare the tofu by carefully turning it out of the packet (run a knife around the edge first) onto a double layer of paper towel. Wrap the tofu in more paper towel and place it on a tray or plate with another plate on top to press for 20 minutes. Gently cut into 5cm cubes.

Heat the oils in a wok over high heat, add the mince and fry until lightly browned. Stir through the chilli bean sauce, black beans, oyster sauce, ginger, Shaoxing wine, caster sugar and Sichuan peppercorns and toss for a few minutes until the sauces are fragrant. Add the stock or dashi and bring to a simmer. Simmer for about 15 minutes, then add the cornflour mixture, stirring until the mixture thickens.

Very gently stir through the tofu without breaking it apart too much and continue to simmer for about 5 minutes until the tofu is warmed through. Stir in the spring onions and serve with steamed rice.

TIP / For an even more authentic Sichuanese flavour, my secret ingredient is a spoon of green Sichuan pepper oil stirred through just before serving. It gives the dish a beautiful fragrance and an extra numbing tingle on the lips. Sichuan pepper oil is sold at Asian supermarkets as 'prickly ash oil'.

# Grandma's tofu

**Mápó tòfu** / This dish is one of the cornerstones of Sichuanese cooking, and it's hugely popular all over the world. It captures the distinctive chilli heat and numbing tingle of Sichuanese cuisine with silky tofu for a dish full of flavour and texture. It may take a trip to an Asian grocer to get your hands on some of the ingredients, but it's worth it.

**Serves** / 6
**Prep** / 20 minutes  **Stand** / 20 minutes  **Cook** / 30 minutes

400g chicken thigh fillets, skin removed and thinly sliced
4 tbsp Chi-Thai Sauce (page 22)
¼ cup Garlic Oil (page 23)
6 spring onions, trimmed and cut into 5cm lengths
2 cups shredded Chinese cabbage
1 large red chilli, sliced
1 kg fresh thick yellow egg (Hokkien) noodles
1 cup basil leaves, loosely packed
Salt, to season
Lemon wedges, to serve

Mix the sliced chicken with half of the Chi-Thai Sauce and set aside for 10 minutes to marinate.

Heat a wok over high heat and add half of the Garlic Oil. Fry the chicken until lightly browned and nearly cooked through, then remove from the oil and set aside. Return the wok to very high heat and add the remainder of the oil, the spring onions, Chinese cabbage and chilli and toss until the cabbage wilts. Add the noodles and the remainder of the Chi-Thai Sauce and toss until the noodles are just starting to soften. Return the chicken to the wok and toss for a few more minutes until the noodles are al dente and the chicken is cooked through. Toss through the basil leaves and a sprinkling of salt if necessary. Serve with lemon wedges.

**TIP** / Just as with pasta, a good noodle dish should be about the noodles. Don't overload noodles with meat or vegetables. A good rule of thumb is that the total weight of meat and vegetables should be between a third to a half of the weight of the fresh noodles.

# Chi-Thai noodles

A simple noodle dish can feed a whole family with just a few ingredients and a minimum of effort. This basic fried noodle recipe can be adapted to just about any meat and vegetable combination. Try replacing cabbage with snow peas, or the chicken with beef or seafood. It is especially good when made with slices of Chinese barbecued duck.

**Serves** / 4
**Prep** / 15 minutes **Marinate** / 10 minutes **Cook** / 10 minutes

- 3 tbsp Garlic Oil (page 23), or 3 cloves garlic, peeled, chopped and fried in 3 tbsp vegetable oil
- 2 chicken thigh fillets, skin off and thinly sliced
- 12 raw prawns, peeled and deveined
- 2 pak choy, trimmed and cut into bite-sized pieces
- 4 spring onions, trimmed and cut into 5cm lengths
- 2 tomatoes, roughly chopped
- 8 fried tofu puffs, halved diagonally
- 1kg fresh thick yellow egg (Hokkien) noodles
- 2 tbsp soy sauce
- 2 tbsp oyster sauce
- 3 tbsp kecap manis
- 1 tbsp tomato sauce
- 1 tsp curry powder
- 3 eggs
- Cucumber and tomato slices, to serve
- Lemon or lime wedges, to serve
- Sliced bird's-eye chillies in soy sauce, to serve

Heat a wok over very high heat and add the Garlic Oil. Add the chicken and fry until just browned. Add the prawns, pak choy and spring onions and toss to coat in the oil. When the prawns change colour, add the tomatoes and tofu puffs. Toss for about 2 minutes, or until the tomatoes and tofu soften.

Add a little more oil if necessary and add the noodles, soy sauce, oyster sauce, kecap manis, tomato sauce and curry powder, tossing in the wok for about 3 minutes until the noodles are softened. Move everything to one side of the wok and crack the eggs directly into the open side. Mix the eggs well and when slightly firm, toss through the noodles. Serve with cucumber and tomato slices, a wedge of lemon or lime, and some sliced chillies in soy sauce on the side.

TIP / Many Malaysians like to serve a bit of sambal belacan as a condiment with their mee goreng. Just pound into a paste a cup of fresh red chillies, 2 tbsp toasted belacan (shrimp paste), a shredded kaffir lime leaf and a teaspoon of sugar. Stir through 2 tbsp lime juice and serve a big spoon of it on the side of your noodles.

# Mee goreng

Mee goreng translates simply as 'fried noodles' in Malay. There are many variations across Malaysia, Indonesia and Singapore, but the version that has really captured hearts abroad is the one available at the mamak stalls of Malaysia, originally created by the South Indian Tamil Muslim communities, with tomato, sweet soy sauce and just a hint of curry spice.

**Serves** / 4
**Prep** / 20 minutes  **Cook** / 10 minutes

600g chicken thigh fillets

4 tbsp Chi-Thai Sauce (page 22) or
4 tbsp oyster sauce

3 tbsp Garlic Oil (page 23) or 3 cloves
garlic, peeled, chopped and fried in
3 tbsp vegetable oil

2 king oyster (eringi) mushrooms,
sliced, or 2 cups halved button
mushrooms

16 snow peas, tailed

1 tbsp cornflour, mixed with 2 tbsp
cold water

Steamed rice, to serve

Slice the chicken thigh fillets in half lengthways and then slice each half diagonally into medallions. Mix with 2 tbsp of the Chi-Thai Sauce or oyster sauce and set aside for 10 minutes to marinate.

Heat a wok over high heat and add the Garlic Oil. Add the chicken and toss in the wok until browned (you may need to do this in batches depending on the size of your wok). Add the mushrooms and toss for about 2 minutes, or until softened. Add the remaining 2 tbsp Chi-Thai Sauce or oyster sauce and the snow peas, as well as a few tablespoons of water if the wok is looking too dry. Toss for another minute, then drizzle in the cornflour mixture very slowly, tossing until the sauce is thickened and sticking to the ingredients, and the snow peas are just barely cooked and still crisp. Transfer to a plate and allow to rest for about a minute. Serve with steamed rice.

**TIP** / Try not to include more than one meat or seafood, or more than three different kinds of vegetables in any stir-fry. Let the natural flavours of those ingredients define the dish, rather than the sauce you cook them with.

# Chicken, mushrooms & snow peas

When stir-frying, simplicity is the key. Adding too many ingredients or heavy sauces to a stir-fried dish will confuse or overpower it. The core flavours of this dish are chicken, mushroom and snow peas. It doesn't need to be any more complicated than that.

**Serves** / 4
**Prep** / 10 minutes **Marinate** / 10 minutes **Cook** / 10 minutes

4 small salmon fillets (about 150g each), pinboned and skin removed

½ cup cornflour

2 cups vegetable oil, for shallow-frying

3 cups mixed Asian mushrooms (such as king oyster or eringi, shimeji, enoki)

1 tsp grated ginger

2 cloves garlic, peeled and minced

4 spring onions, trimmed and sliced diagonally

¼ head iceberg lettuce, cut into 5cm-wide strips

2 tbsp oyster sauce

1 tbsp soy sauce

1 tbsp Shaoxing wine

1 tbsp rice vinegar

½ tsp sesame oil

½ tsp sugar

2 cups Cabbage Dashi (page 17) or Whole Chicken Stock (page 18)

1 tbsp cornflour, mixed with 2 tbsp cold water

Steamed rice, to serve

Dust the salmon in cornflour and shake off any excess. Put 2cm oil in the base of a wok or frypan and heat it to 180°C. Shallow-fry the salmon for about 2 minutes each side until barely cooked. Keep warm in a very low oven until ready to use.

Clean the wok or frypan and heat an additional 1 tbsp oil over high heat. Tear or slice the mushrooms into bite-sized pieces and fry, tossing occasionally until the mushrooms are softened and browned. Add the ginger, garlic, onions and lettuce and toss together. Add the oyster sauce, soy sauce, Shaoxing wine, vinegar, sesame oil, sugar and dashi or stock and bring to a simmer. Simmer for about 5 minutes, or until the lettuce is wilted. Add the cornflour mixture in a thin stream while stirring and simmer for a further minute until the sauce thickens.

Arrange the salmon on a serving plate with a lip and pour over the sauce. Serve with rice.

TIP / You can leave the skin on if you prefer. Score it at 5mm intervals and fry the fish skin-side first for about 3 minutes until the skin crisps.

# Salmon with braised mushrooms & lettuce

The earthiness of salmon is a great match with mushrooms of any kind. This dish combines the crisp-fried fish with a luxurious sauce of braised mushrooms. The iceberg lettuce becomes silky smooth when cooked, retaining just a hint of its crunch. Together, it's a great combination.

**Serves** / 4
**Prep** / 20 minutes  **Cook** / 20 minutes

500g pork mince

4 tbsp Chi-Thai Sauce (page 22) or
2 tbsp oyster sauce mixed with
2 tbsp fish sauce and ½ tsp
caster sugar

3 tbsp Garlic Oil (page 23) or 3 cloves
garlic, peeled, chopped and fried
in 3 tbsp vegetable oil

250g green beans, trimmed and cut
into 5cm lengths

2 large red chillies, sliced

2 kaffir lime leaves, central vein
removed and very finely sliced

Steamed rice, to serve

Mix the pork mince with 2 tbsp of the Chi-Thai Sauce or 1 tbsp of oyster sauce mixture and set aside for 10 minutes to marinate.

Heat a wok over high heat and add the Garlic Oil. Add the kaffir lime leaves and fry for just a few seconds until they are bright green and crisp, then remove from the wok and set aside. Add the pork to the wok and toss while breaking it apart until browned. Add the green beans, chillies and remaining 2 tbsp Chi-Thai Sauce or the oyster sauce mixture and toss for about 2 minutes, or until the beans are softened. Stir through the kaffir lime leaves and remove from the heat. Transfer to a plate and allow to rest for about a minute. Serve with steamed rice.

TIP / You can make any number of variations on this dish simply by replacing the kaffir lime with another flavour. Black beans, chilli bean paste, dried Chinese olives and Tianjin preserved vegetables are available from Asian supermarkets and all work well in this dish.

# Pork, green beans & lime leaf

Pork with green beans is a great combination found in a lot of Chinese dishes. This dish incorporates a few fresh Thai flavours into the mix. I prefer the beans crisp, but if you like them soft as is often preferred in Chinese cuisine (they are sometimes deep-fried first), add them to the wok before the pork mince and fry them a little longer.

**Serves** / 4
**Prep** / 10 minutes **Marinate** / 10 minutes **Cook** / 10 minutes

1½ cups kimchi
1 tbsp vegetable oil
1 tbsp sesame oil
1 tbsp gochujang (Korean chilli
    bean paste)
4 cups cooked jasmine or
    short-grain rice
3 spring onions, trimmed and
    finely sliced
1 tsp salt
1 tbsp toasted sesame seeds
4 small sheets Korean nori, crumbled
    (or 1 sheet Japanese nori, toasted
    and crumbled)

Squeeze as much juice as you can from the kimchi, then finely slice it and set aside, reserving the juice.

Heat a wok over high heat and add the vegetable oil and sesame oil. Add the kimchi to the wok and toss frequently until very fragrant. Add the gochujang and toss for about a minute, or until fragrant.

Add the rice, pressing it onto the sides of the wok to separate the grains. Add the reserved kimchi juice, spring onions and salt, and mix everything well, allowing the rice to lightly toast against the sides of the wok.

Scatter the rice with sesame seeds and crumbled nori and serve.

TIP / Korean nori is available from Asian supermarkets often roasted with sesame oil and salted, and is easily crumbled. I keep a pack or two in my pantry at all times. It makes a great snack.

# Kimchi fried rice

If you're like me and always keep a tub of kimchi in the fridge, this is one of those weeknight dishes that's perfect when there isn't much else around. You'd be surprised how tasty and satisfying a bowl of this economical fried rice can be.

**Serves** / 4
**Prep** / 10 minutes  **Cook** / 10 minutes

800g boneless lamb leg, sliced into
    bite-sized pieces
2 tsp baking soda (optional)
2 tbsp cornflour
3 tbsp vegetable oil
1 green capsicum, deseeded and
    thinly sliced
6 spring onions, trimmed and cut
    into 5cm lengths
1 tsp grated ginger
¼ cup Chi-Thai Sauce (page 22) or
    2 tbsp oyster sauce mixed
    with 2 tbsp dark soy sauce,
    2 tbsp Shaoxing wine and 1 tsp
    caster sugar
1 tbsp hoisin sauce
Steamed rice, to serve

To tenderise the lamb like they do in Chinese restaurants, mix the baking soda with 2 tbsp cold water to a slurry. Pour over the sliced lamb and mix well. Allow to stand for 30 minutes then rinse the lamb very well, then rinse again and pat dry. If you don't want to tenderise the lamb, just skip this step.

Toss the lamb and cornflour together. Add the vegetable oil to a hot wok and fry the lamb in batches over high heat until it is well browned all over. Set aside on a warm plate. Add a little more oil to the wok if necessary and fry the capsicum and spring onion until they start to soften. Add the ginger, sauces and lamb (including any juices that have come out of the lamb while resting) and toss well for a minute or two, or until the sauces thicken and coat the lamb. Serve with steamed rice.

TIP / Tenderising meat with baking soda works best with tougher cuts of beef and lamb. Be sure to wash the baking soda off the meat completely or it can give the meat an unpleasant dry or fizzy taste.

# Mongolian lamb

The sweet sauce coating the tender lamb in this dish brings back a lot of memories for me, from ordering it in suburban Chinese restaurants when I was a kid. Since then I've learned that nobody in Mongolia eats lamb this way, but that doesn't mean we can't still enjoy it.

Serves / 4–6
Prep / 20 minutes  Stand / 30 minutes (optional)  Cook / 10 minutes

¼ cup vegetable oil

1 large eggplant, halved and sliced in thick strips

1 long red chilli, finely chopped

4 cloves garlic, peeled and finely chopped

1 tsp grated ginger

500g pork mince

3 tbsp oyster sauce

1 tbsp dark soy sauce

1 tsp caster sugar

1 cup water or Whole Chicken Stock (page 18)

1 tsp cornflour, mixed with 1 tbsp cold water

2 spring onions, trimmed and finely chopped

Steamed rice, to serve

Heat 2 tbsp oil in a wok and fry the eggplant over medium heat in batches until well browned. Set aside.

Heat the remaining oil in the wok and add the chilli, garlic and ginger and fry until fragrant. Add the mince, break it apart in the wok and toss until browned. Add the oyster sauce, soy sauce, sugar and water or stock and bring to a simmer. Add the eggplant and simmer for about 8 minutes, or until the eggplant is tender. Gradually add the cornflour mixture while stirring until any liquid is thickened. Scatter with spring onions and serve with steamed rice.

**TIP** / Eggplant will absorb a lot of oil when it is first fried, but as it cooks and softens some of that oil will be released back into the sauce. Don't be tempted to add too much oil at the beginning or your sauce will end up too oily.

# Pork & eggplant

This is one of those dishes that just makes you want to grab a bowl and curl up in front of the television. As far as comfort food goes in Asia, this is the sofa and the slippers.

**Serves** / 4
**Prep** / 10 minutes  **Cook** / 15 minutes

4 tbsp vegetable oil

¼ cup Tom Yum Paste (page 23) or commercial paste

200g chicken thigh fillets, thinly sliced

8 large raw prawns, peeled, deveined and sliced in half lengthways

1 small red onion, peeled and thinly sliced

½ cup sliced button mushrooms

½ cup sliced green beans (1cm lengths)

8 cups cooked jasmine rice

2 tbsp fish sauce

½ cup cherry tomatoes, quartered

1 cup coriander leaves, to serve

Lemon wedges, to serve

Heat a wok over high heat and add the vegetable oil and Tom Yum Paste. Fry the paste until fragrant and add the chicken slices and prawns, tossing in the wok for a few minutes until they are about half cooked through.

Add the onion, mushrooms and beans and toss for a further minute to soften the vegetables. Add a little more oil if you need (the mushrooms can soak up a lot of the oil) and add the rice, pressing it onto the sides of the wok to separate the grains. Add the fish sauce and cherry tomatoes and toss over high heat until the rice is warmed through and the ingredients are well mixed. Scatter with the coriander leaves and serve with lemon wedges.

TIP / In Asian households fried rice is eaten on its own either as a complete meal or as a separate course. It's not usually eaten as an accompaniment to other dishes.

# Tom yum fried rice

Fried rice is an easy way to feed a hungry family. Just a few ingredients can go a long way, and there are versions all over Asia, from Indonesian nasi goreng to Japanese chahan. This Thai tom yum version puts the familiar soup flavours in a fried rice form.

**Serves** / 4–6
**Prep** / 20 minutes  **Cook** / 10 minutes

big
pot

1 tbsp oil
4 chicken Marylands
2 onions, peeled and diced
4 cloves garlic, peeled and chopped
1 tbsp grated ginger
1 tbsp each of ground turmeric, cumin and coriander
1 tsp chilli powder, or to taste
1 tsp salt
1 can (400g) diced tomatoes
1 can (400ml) coconut milk
Juice of ½ lemon
1 cup coriander leaves, to serve
Steamed rice, to serve

Heat the oil in a heavy pot over high heat. Cut three or four deep slits into each of the chicken pieces (across the bone) and fry, two at a time, until well browned. Remove from the pot and set aside.

Reduce the heat to medium and add a little more oil to the pot if necessary. Fry the onion until softened, then add the garlic and ginger and continue to fry until fragrant. Add the turmeric, cumin, coriander, chilli and salt and stir well to combine. Add the tomatoes and coconut milk, stir well, and return the chicken to the pot, covering the joints with the rich curry sauce. Bring the pot to the boil, reduce the heat and simmer, covered, for 20–30 minutes, or until the chicken is very tender. Uncover the pot and allow to stand for 10 minutes, then if you have time, cover the pot again and allow it to cool to room temperature. Reheat when ready to serve (see Tip).

Squeeze over the lemon juice, scatter over the coriander leaves and serve the Kuku Paka with rice, and some Ajat (page 228) if you like.

**TIP** / Allowing a dish to cool and then reheating it allows flavours to develop at different temperatures. If you've ever thought that curries taste better the day after they're cooked, this simple process will give you a similar result in a much shorter time.

# Kuku paka

This African dish is one of the easiest curries you could ever make. Kuku is Swahili for 'chicken', and paka is the Bengali word for 'delicious'. Names aside, if you're looking for a simple one-pot dish with big flavour, this will soon be a regular on your kitchen roster.

**Serves** / 4
**Prep** / 10 minutes  **Cook** / 40 minutes  **Stand** / 10 minutes

2 litres water or Cabbage Dashi
(page 17), Prawn Stock (page 18)
or Whole Chicken Stock (page 18)
3 tbsp sake
2kg live mussels
½ cup miso paste
1 block (300g) silken tofu, drained
and cut into 2cm cubes
3 spring onions, trimmed and finely
sliced
3 cups baby spinach leaves
Steamed rice, to serve (optional)

Bring the water, dashi or stock to the boil with the sake in a large saucepan and drop in the mussels in batches in a strainer, boiling each batch for 2 minutes, then removing them as the mussels open. Divide the cooked mussels across four bowls and return the soup to the boil.

Turn off the heat and place the miso paste in the strainer. Partially submerge the strainer in the soup and work the miso through to dissolve it into the soup. Discard any solid pieces of soy bean, husk or grit left in the strainer. Once the miso has been added, do not return the soup to the boil at any stage. Taste the soup and adjust the flavour by adding more miso if necessary.

Stir through the tofu, spring onions and baby spinach leaves and divide the soup between the bowls. Serve immediately, with rice if you wish.

TIP / You can also add noodles to this dish if you wish. Just boil the noodles first in plain water and place them in the bowls before you add the mussels. Always boil noodles separately for soupy noodle dishes because the flour coating the noodles can cloud and affect the consistency of the soup.

# Big miso soup with mussels

This meal-sized miso soup is a fantastic way to get the most out of your mussels. Steaming mussels is quick and easy, but often the steaming process can result in uneven cooking. Boiling the mussels in this recipe ensures they are evenly cooked, perfectly tender, and produce a delicious and healthy soup.

**Serves** / 4
**Prep** / 10 minutes **Cook** / 10 minutes

8 dried shiitake mushrooms

400g skinless pork belly, shoulder or leg, thinly sliced

3 tbsp oyster sauce

2 tbsp fish sauce

2 tbsp dark soy sauce

1 tsp cornflour

1 tsp sesame oil

¼ cup Garlic Oil (page 23) or 3 cloves garlic, peeled, chopped and fried in 3 tbsp vegetable oil

1 tbsp grated ginger

2–3 large Chinese cabbage leaves, roughly shredded

6 spring onions, trimmed and cut diagonally into 5cm lengths

150g enoki mushrooms, trimmed

A pinch of caster sugar

1½ cups Whole Chicken Stock (page 18) or Cabbage Dashi (page 17)

400g dried rice vermicelli noodles, soaked in cold water for 30 minutes, and drained

1 tbsp cornflour, mixed with 2 tbsp cold water (optional)

**CHILLI & CUMQUAT**

2 tsp soy sauce

2 red bird's-eye chillies, sliced

3 juicy cumquats, roughly chopped, or 2 tsp lemon juice

Reconstitute the shiitake mushrooms in 2 cups boiling water for 30 minutes, then remove and discard the stalks, and slice the caps. Reserve the steeping liquid.

Meanwhile, mix together the sliced pork with one tablespoon each of the oyster sauce, fish sauce and dark soy sauce, and add the cornflour and sesame oil. Set aside to marinate for 5 minutes.

Heat the Garlic Oil in a large pot over high heat. Add the pork and fry until lightly browned. Add the ginger, Chinese cabbage, spring onions, enoki mushrooms and sliced shiitake mushrooms. Stir occasionally until the vegetables are softened, then stir through the remaining oyster sauce, fish sauce, dark soy sauce and sugar.

Add half the reserved shiitake steeping liquid and the stock or dashi. Bring to the boil and taste the liquid. It should be strongly flavoured and salty.

Add the drained noodles and stir through. Simmer for 2–3 minutes, or until the noodles are soft and have absorbed the stock. If there is still a lot of liquid around the noodles, add the cornflour and water mixture and stir until thickened. Remove from the heat and let stand for a few minutes before serving.

For the chilli and cumquat, mix the ingredients together and lightly squash the chunks of cumquat to release their sweet juice. Serve the noodles with the chilli and cumquat on the side.

TIP / Cumquats have a very thin pith and few seeds so they can be eaten whole, rind and all. My grandmother regularly makes the chilli and cumquat condiment using cumquats from our garden. Their sweet flesh, juice and rind brightens the flavours of the chilli.

# Big pot noodles

These noodles are great for feeding a crowd. Just throw everything into a big pot (in the right order, mind you!) and you'll be rewarded with a seemingly endless amount of delicious noodles. The secret is in the sauce. Pack the pot with ingredients to make the sauce delicious, and as the noodles soak it all up they'll be delicious, too.

**Serves** / 6
**Prep** / 20 minutes **Soak** / 30 minutes **Cook** / 20 minutes

1 whole baby snapper (about 700g), cleaned and scaled, or 600g boneless red snapper fillets

1 tsp sesame oil

Salt, to season

3 cups short-grain rice, washed and drained

4 cups cold water

1 tbsp fish sauce

3 tbsp sake

2 tbsp soy sauce

2cm ginger, peeled and cut into fine matchsticks

½ tsp salt flakes

2 spring onions, trimmed and finely sliced

2 tsp toasted sesame seeds

Wash the snapper under running water and pat dry with paper towel. If using a whole fish make 3–4 thick diagonal cuts to the bone along each side. Rub the skin with sesame oil and season well with salt. Heat a barbecue, frypan or overhead grill until very hot and toast the fish on each side until lightly browned. (The fish does not need to be cooked through.) If grilling, wrap the tail of the fish in aluminium foil so it doesn't burn.

Place the rice and water in a heavy-based pot, then add the fish sauce, sake and soy sauce. Place the fish on top of the rice and scatter both the rice and fish with the ginger.

Bring the pot to the boil over medium heat, uncovered, and when boiling vigorously cover the pot and reduce the heat to very low. Keep on very low heat for 15 minutes then turn off the heat and allow the pot to stand for a further 5 minutes.

Remove the snapper from the pot and with two forks or a pair of chopsticks, roughly shred the skin and flesh from the bones. Discard all the bones and return the skin and flesh to the rice. Scatter with the salt flakes and carefully stir the fish through the rice.

Serve with a sprinkling of spring onions and sesame seeds. This is excellent accompanied by Basic Miso Soup (page 225), Ginger-pickled Cucumber (page 224) and Red Radish Pickles (page 224).

TIP / Even if you buy your fish already scaled, it's a good habit to give it a once-over with a scaler or the back of a knife yourself when you get it home. Fishmongers sometimes miss scaling the head of whole fish.

# Snapper rice

It's almost biblical how this dish takes one small fish and a few cups of rice to feed a whole family. What is most amazing, though, is how just a few selected ingredients can combine to produce such a powerful flavour in a dish so simple, light and delicate.

**Serves** / 4
**Prep** / 10 minutes  **Cook** / 30 minutes

2 tsp black peppercorns

1 tsp salt

1 tbsp Chinese five spice powder

10 cloves garlic, peeled

Stems and roots from 3 roots of coriander, finely chopped, leaves reserved

2 tbsp vegetable oil

4kg pork leg, skin on

¼ cup fish sauce

¼ cup soy sauce

2 tbsp dark soy sauce

2 tbsp sugar

2 star anise

2 cinnamon sticks

6–8 Steamed Eggs (page 228) or hard-boiled eggs, peeled

Steamed rice and green vegetables, to serve

**CHILLI & GARLIC VINEGAR**

½ cup white vinegar

4 garlic cloves, peeled and finely chopped

2 bird's-eye chillies, finely chopped

Reserved leaves from 3 coriander roots, finely shredded

3 tsp caster sugar

1 tsp salt

In a mortar and pestle or food processor, pound or process the peppercorns, salt, five spice, garlic and coriander roots and stems to a rough paste.

Heat the oil in a very large pot and brown the pork leg on all sides. Cover the pork with cold water and add the peppercorn paste, fish sauce, soy sauce, dark soy sauce, sugar, star anise and cinnamon. Bring the pot to a simmer, and continue to simmer, covered, for 3–4 hours, or until the meat is very tender and falling off the bone. Remove from the heat and add the Steamed Eggs to the pot, ensuring they are completely covered with liquid.

To make the chilli and garlic vinegar, combine all the ingredients and stir until the sugar is dissolved.

Shred the pork into large chunks, halve the eggs and serve with rice, greens and the chilli and garlic vinegar on the side.

**TIP** / This dish freezes really well. Just cover the shredded meat with plenty of braising liquid in a freezer bag or plastic container. It will keep for a few months.

# Thai-style braised pork

**Khao kha mu** / One of the most popular dishes sold by street vendors in Thailand, Khao kha mu is usually made with pork hock, trading off the rich textures of gelatinous skin and fat to complement the tender meat. I prefer pork leg because it is a little leaner, but I still keep some of the fat and skin in the mix.

**Serves** / 8–10

**Prep** / 30 minutes  **Cook** / 3–4 hours

¼ cup vegetable oil

1½ cups Easy Red Curry Paste (page 24) or commercial paste

1 can (400ml) coconut cream

1½ litres Whole Chicken Stock (page 18) or water

4 tbsp fish sauce

1 tbsp sugar

4 kaffir lime leaves

1 eggplant, halved lengthways and sliced

1 zucchini, halved lengthways and sliced

1 red capsicum, deseeded and cut into strips

1 red onion, peeled and cut into chunks

8 spears baby corn, halved

2 cups button mushrooms, halved

1 cup green beans, trimmed and cut into 5cm lengths

2 cups cherry tomatoes

1kg beef topside, sliced very thinly (see Tip)

1 cup loosely packed basil leaves

30ml lime juice (about 1 lime)

Coriander leaves, to serve

Steamed rice, to serve

Heat the oil in a large pot and fry the curry paste over medium heat for about 10 minutes, stirring occasionally until the paste is very fragrant. Add the coconut cream and continue to fry for a further 5 minutes. Add the stock or water and bring to the boil. Add the fish sauce, sugar and lime leaves. Simmer for about 10 minutes, or until the top of the liquid starts to take on an oily shine.

Add the vegetables and return to a simmer for 5 minutes, or until they begin to soften, then add the beef and simmer for a further 5 minutes, or until cooked through. Stir through the basil leaves and lime juice. Scatter with coriander leaves and serve with steamed rice.

TIP / You can make this recipe with any kind of meat or seafood. It's particularly good with the meat and skin from a whole Chinese barbecue duck, or even a shop-bought barbecue chicken. If you have any Shredded Chicken (page 18) or meat left over from a Sunday roast, they make for a great curry, too. Perhaps even try prawns, substituting the Whole Chicken Stock with Prawn Stock (page 18) as well.

# Big red curry

Thai curries like this one are usually cooked quickly and that's perfect for a meal to feed a big crowd. It's great as soon as it's ready and the vegetables have a bit of crunch, but it's almost better as leftovers. After the pot has been heated and cooled a few times the flavours develop and the vegetables soften further, like in a stew.

**Serves** / 6–8
**Prep** / 30 minutes **Cook** / 40 minutes

3 sebago potatoes, peeled and cut into chunks
2 tbsp unsalted butter
2 tbsp olive oil
600g chicken thigh fillets, skin removed and cut into slices
1 brown onion, peeled, halved and cut into 1cm slices
¼ Chinese cabbage, cut into 5cm lengths
150g oyster mushrooms
1 tsp salt, plus extra, to season
½ cup plain flour
2 cups milk
4 cups Cabbage Dashi (page 17) or Whole Chicken Stock (page 18)
½ tsp white pepper
¼ cup finely chopped chives, to serve

Boil the potatoes in boiling salted water for 10 minutes, or until nearly tender. Drain and set aside.

Heat a large saucepan over medium heat, add the butter and oil and fry the chicken until lightly cooked but not browned. Add the onion, cabbage, mushrooms and salt and stir until the vegetables are softened and have released their liquid. Stir through the flour and fry for about 3–4 minutes, or until the mixture is thickened. Add the milk and bring to a simmer, stirring constantly. Then add the potatoes and dashi or stock and bring to a simmer again, stirring frequently. Simmer for about 10 minutes, or until the stew is thick and all the vegetables are soft.

Season with salt to taste, scatter over the white pepper and chives and serve.

TIP / A popular variation on this dish in Japan is the doria. Place some steamed rice in a gratin dish, top with the stew and scatter with cheese. Grill under an overhead grill until the cheese is melted and browned, and serve.

# White
## stew

Stews don't always have to be heavy, brown and cooked for hours. This Japanese white stew is light, clean and ready in a fraction of the time. It tastes fantastic, too.

**Serves** / 4
**Prep** / 15 minutes  **Cook** / 30 minutes

- 600g wagyu beef sirloin, very thinly sliced (see Tip)
- 700g sebago potatoes, peeled and cut into irregular chunks
- 2 carrots, peeled and cut into irregular chunks
- 1 large brown onion, peeled, halved and cut into 1cm slices
- 15 snow peas, tailed
- Steamed rice, to serve

**NIKUJAGA STOCK**
- 3 cups Cabbage Dashi (page 17)
- ½ cup soy sauce
- ¼ cup sake
- ¼ cup mirin
- ¼ cup caster sugar

Bring the ingredients for the stock to a simmer then add the beef slices, stir and simmer for about 2 minutes, or until the beef is just cooked through. Remove the beef from the pot and set aside, covered.

Return the stock to a simmer and skim any scum from the top of the liquid. Add the potatoes and carrots and cover the top of the pot with baking paper laid directly on top of the ingredients. Simmer for about 10 minutes then add the onion. Re-cover with the baking paper and simmer for a further 10 minutes, or until the potato and carrots are tender and the onion is cooked.

Stir the beef through the vegetables and simmer, uncovered, for a further 10 minutes, or until most of the liquid is evaporated and the meat and vegetables have softened. Allow the mixture to rest and cool for at least 30 minutes. Reheat the meat and potatoes on the stove when ready to serve.

In a separate pot of boiling salted water, blanch the snow peas for 1 minute and drain. Stir the snow peas through the meat and potatoes and serve with steamed rice.

**TIP** / To slice beef very thinly put it in the freezer until it is firm then slice with a sharp knife. Thinly sliced beef and other meats are also available from Asian butchers, and frozen in Asian grocers.

# Nikujaga

The name of this Japanese dish translates to 'meat and potatoes', and it is considered a staple of the Japanese home kitchen. Every Japanese family will have their own version. This is how we make it in our family, as taught to me by my mother-in-law.

**Serves** / 4
**Prep** / 20 minutes **Cook** / 25 minutes **Rest** / 30 minutes

2kg lamb leg meat, cut into 4cm cubes
¼ cup vegetable oil
2 onions, peeled and finely chopped
Steamed rice, to serve
Cucumber Raita (page 227), to serve
Tomato Salad (page 227), to serve

## VINDALOO PASTE
1 tsp mustard powder
2 tbsp chilli powder
2 tbsp ground cumin
1 tsp ground cinnamon
2 tsp black pepper
2 cups dry white wine
1 cup white vinegar
¼ cup caster sugar
12 cloves garlic
2 tbsp grated ginger
1 onion, peeled and roughly chopped

Combine the paste ingredients in a blender or food processor and blend to a smooth paste. Pour the paste over the lamb in a non-reactive bowl and marinate for at least 3 hours.

Heat a little of the oil in a large pot over high heat until very hot. Remove the lamb from the marinade, leaving behind as much of the reserved marinade and meat juices as possible. Fry the lamb in batches until well browned, adding extra oil as necessary, and set aside. Fry the onions in a little more of the oil until golden brown and return the browned lamb to the pot. Add the reserved marinade plus half a cup of water, reduce the heat to low and simmer, uncovered, for 1 hour, or until the lamb is very tender. If the vindaloo starts to look too dry, add a little extra water or cover the pot with a lid. Serve with rice, Cucumber Raita and Tomato Salad.

TIP / Although vindaloo is great with lamb, it was originally made with pork. Substitute cubes of pork leg or shoulder for the lamb for something different, or even try this with chuck steak.

# Lamb
# vindaloo

It might come as a surprise that lamb vindaloo has Portuguese origins. Portuguese vinha d'alhos crossed the world with the explorers, and now pops up everywhere in various forms, from Filipino adobo and Trinidadian garlic pork to Hawaiian pork and vinegar and, of course, Goan vindaloo. In Goa, the traditional flavourings of wine, garlic and vinegar get a workover with Indian spices.

**Serves** / 6–8
**Prep** / 25 minutes **Marinate** / 3 hours **Cook** / 1 hour 10 minutes

2 potatoes, peeled and cut into chunks
1 daikon radish, peeled and cut
   into chunks
2 carrots, peeled and cut into chunks
½ Chinese cabbage, cut into 5cm
   pieces
10 fresh shiitake mushrooms,
   stalks removed
300g enoki mushrooms, trimmed
6 spring onions, trimmed and sliced
   diagonally
1 block (300g) firm tofu, drained
   and cut into large cubes
600g chicken thigh fillets
2 salmon fillets (about 180g each),
   skin and bones removed and cut
   into thick slices
2 tbsp toasted sesame seeds, roughly
   ground, to serve

**SOUP BASE**
1 litre Whole Chicken Stock (page 18)
1 litre Cabbage Dashi (page 17)
2 tbsp soy sauce
2 tbsp mirin
2 tbsp sake
1 tsp salt
1 tsp caster sugar

Place the potato, daikon and carrot in a large pot and cover with cold water. Bring the pot to the boil and simmer for 10 minutes. Drain the water and set the parboiled vegetables aside.

In a very large pot, bring the soup base ingredients to a simmer, add the Chinese cabbage, mushrooms, parboiled root vegetables and spring onions and return to a simmer. Add the tofu, chicken and salmon, cover the pot and cook for about 10 minutes, or until the chicken and salmon are cooked through and the vegetables are softened. Adjust for seasoning, scatter with sesame seeds and serve.

**TIP** / At chanko nabe restaurants in Japan a large pot of soup base is brought to a simmer at the table and the other ingredients are piled into a giant bowl for guests to add to the soup as they like. If you have a portable burner that can be put on your dining table, you could try this method for an interactive family dinner.

# Sumo stew

**Chanko nabe** / This is classic sumo food. You might think those giants just pile on the calories, but this dish is actually light, healthy and low in fat. There's no fixed recipe for it – versions can contain beef, prawns, pork, mussels or anything you like. This one uses chicken and salmon, but don't be afraid to throw in whatever takes your fancy.

**Serves** / 6
**Prep** / 20 minutes  **Cook** / 30 minutes

1 tbsp butter
1 tbsp olive oil
1 large onion, peeled and finely diced
3 cloves garlic, peeled and finely
    chopped
1½ tbsp curry powder
1 tsp garam masala
2 tsp salt
1 can (400g) diced tomatoes
1½ litres Whole Chicken Stock
    (page 18)
½ cup washed uncooked brown rice
    or jasmine rice
1 Granny Smith apple, peeled and
    finely diced
1 carrot, peeled and finely diced
1 small sweet potato, peeled and
    finely diced
2 cups Shredded Chicken (page 18)
    (optional)
1 cup Greek-style yoghurt, to serve
    (optional)
Roughly chopped coriander leaves,
    to serve

Heat the butter and olive oil in a large pot over medium heat and fry the onion and garlic until softened. Add the curry powder, garam masala, salt and tomatoes and fry for a minute, or until the spices are fragrant.

Add the chicken stock and rice and simmer, covered, for 1½ hours, stirring occasionally. Add the apple, carrot and sweet potato and simmer for a further 30 minutes. Adjust for seasoning with a little salt if necessary.

Stir through the Shredded Chicken, if using. Stir through a spoonful of yoghurt (if using) and scatter with chopped coriander to serve.

TIP / Leaving out the chicken and substituting Cabbage Dashi (page 17) (minus the fish sauce) for the Whole Chicken Stock will produce an excellent vegetarian soup.

# Mulligatawny soup

The key to a good Mulligatawny Soup is the combination of the warmth of Indian spices with the sweet and tart Granny Smith apples. I like to cook the rice long and low, almost to a congee consistency. Just a half cup of rice thickens a whole pot of soup from a starter to a hearty meal. It's perfect for when the weather starts to cool.

**Serves** / 6
**Prep** / 20 minutes  **Cook** / 2½ hours

6 ears of corn, husk and silk removed

1½ litres Whole Chicken Stock
   (page 18)

1 litre water

4 thick slices of ginger, unpeeled

1½ tsp salt

1 tbsp soy sauce

2 tbsp Shaoxing wine

2 tbsp cornflour, mixed with 3 tbsp
   cold water

4 eggs, beaten

2–3 cups Shredded Chicken (page 18)

2 spring onions, trimmed and
   thinly sliced

1 tbsp sesame oil

White pepper, to serve

Stand the corn on their ends and run a sharp knife down the sides to remove the kernels. Set the kernels aside and reserve the cobs.

Bring the stock and water to a simmer in a large pot and add the cobs, ginger slices, salt, soy sauce and Shaoxing wine. Simmer the stock covered for 45 minutes, then discard the corn cobs and ginger slices.

Add the reserved kernels and simmer for a further 5 minutes. Taste the soup and adjust the seasoning if necessary. Whisk through the cornflour mixture while simmering the soup until it thickens to a silky consistency.

Continue simmering the soup and add the eggs in a thin stream, whisking slowly but constantly. The eggs should form thin, wispy threads as they cook. Remove from the heat and stir through the Shredded Chicken.

Scatter the soup with sliced spring onions, drizzle with sesame oil and dust with a little white pepper to serve.

TIP / You can make a simple Chinese egg flower soup (also sometimes called 'egg drop soup') using this same method. Bring some Whole Chicken Stock to a simmer without the corn and add the seasonings used in this recipe. Stir through the eggs using the method described then add chopped spring onions and cubes of silken tofu.

# Chinese chicken & corn soup

If you've only ever had this classic Chinese restaurant soup made with canned corn, you are missing out. There is an elegance to extracting all the essence from both the chicken and the fresh corn that gives this soup both flavour and soul.

**Serves** / 4
**Prep** / 10 minutes **Cook** / 1 hour

2 tbsp sesame oil

500g beef or pork mince

3 tbsp gochujang (Korean chilli bean paste)

½ tsp salt

2 tbsp mirin

4 cups kimchi, including juice

4 spring onions, trimmed and cut into 5cm lengths diagonally

1½ litres water or Whole Chicken Stock (page 18)

3 frankfurters, cut into 10cm lengths and cut ¾ of the way through at ½cm intervals

1 block (300g) silken tofu, drained and thickly sliced

2 cups bean sprouts

2 dried noodle cakes, or the noodles only from 2 packets of instant noodles

Steamed rice, to serve

Heat the sesame oil in a wide pot and fry the mince over high heat until browned. Add the gochujang, salt and mirin and stir until mixed with the beef. Add the kimchi, spring onions and water or stock and bring to the boil. Add the frankfurters and simmer for 10 minutes.

Add the sliced tofu, bean sprouts and noodle cakes and cook for a further 3 minutes without stirring, or until the noodles are softened. Serve with steamed rice.

**TIP** / This is a great dish for using up leftovers. If you have any spare vegetables, meats or leftover pasta or noodles, just throw them into the pot.

# Army stew

**Budae chigae** / Originally a way of using surplus US military supplies after the Korean War, budae chigae ('army stew') is now a cheap and cheerful favourite among Korea's younger generations, and anyone wanting to feed a crowd for a song. There's no fixed recipe, and many versions take things to the extreme, adding tinned luncheon meats, baked beans and even slices of cheese. I prefer to keep things simple.

**Serves** / 6
**Prep** / 20 minutes  **Cook** / 20 minutes

2 tbsp vegetable oil
1 onion, peeled and finely chopped
2 tbsp grated ginger
3 cloves garlic, peeled and grated
2 tbsp curry powder
1 tsp garam masala
½ tsp chilli powder
500g lamb mince
1 tsp salt
1 tsp sugar
1 can (400g) diced tomatoes
1 cup water
1 cup frozen peas
1 tbsp butter
1 cup coriander leaves, shredded,
    to serve
Cucumber Raita (page 227), to serve

Heat the oil in a medium saucepan over medium heat. Add the onion, ginger and garlic and fry for 2 minutes, or until fragrant. Add the curry powder, garam masala and chilli powder and fry for about a minute. Add the lamb mince and fry until the mince is browned. Then add the salt, sugar, tomatoes and water and bring to the boil. Simmer, covered, for 45 minutes, then stir through the peas and butter and remove from the heat. Allow the curry to cool, and then reheat to serve.

Scatter the curry with shredded coriander and serve with Cucumber Raita.

**TIP** / This curry also works very well with beef mince. Any leftovers are also great as a filling for making Okonomipotato (page 187).

# Lamb kheema curry

This simple mince curry is delicious, and it really does stretch a long way when feeding a family. It goes perfectly with rice for a great one-bowl, comfort food dinner. Make a double batch as it freezes well.

**Serves** / 4
**Prep** / 15 minutes **Cook** / 1 hour

2 carrots, peeled and quartered

1 ear of corn, husk and silk removed, cut into thick rings

1 eggplant, cut into thick wedges lengthways

1 green capsicum, deseeded and cut into 5cm strips

2 king oyster (eringi) mushrooms, halved lengthways (or quartered if very thick)

4 tbsp vegetable or olive oil

1 tsp salt flakes

4 chicken Marylands, skin removed

1 brown onion, peeled and grated

2 tsp Garlic Paste (page 23) or 2 cloves garlic, peeled and finely chopped

1 tbsp grated ginger

1 tbsp ground cumin

1 tbsp ground coriander

1 tbsp paprika

1 tsp garam masala

1 cinnamon stick

½ cup tomato passata

1 bay leaf

1½ litres water, Whole Chicken Stock (page 18) or Cabbage Dashi (page 17)

1 tbsp soy sauce

1 tbsp sake

1 tbsp mirin

½ cup loosely packed basil leaves, roughly torn

2 Steamed Eggs (page 228) or hard-boiled eggs, halved

Steamed rice or thickly sliced, buttered bread, to serve

Heat the oven to 190°C (fan-forced). Toss the vegetables in 2 tbsp of the oil and arrange on a baking tray lined with baking paper. Scatter with salt and bake the vegetables, uncovered, for 25–30 minutes, or until they are roasted and tender.

Meanwhile, season the chicken Marylands with salt and brown, two at a time, in a little oil in a large pot over high heat then set aside. Add the onion, Garlic Paste and ginger to the pot and fry over medium heat for about 2 minutes, or until softened (add a little more oil if you need to). Add the spices, tomato passata and bay leaf and fry for a further minute until fragrant. Add the water or stock, soy sauce, sake and mirin and bring to a simmer. Return the chicken to the pot and simmer for 30 minutes, or until the chicken is tender. Stir through the basil leaves.

Place each chicken Maryland in a bowl and add the roasted vegetables and half a steamed egg. Pour over the curry soup and serve with steamed rice or thick sliced, buttered bread.

TIP / If you don't want to roast the vegetables, you can boil or steam them, or slice them thinly and pan-fry or grill them. It's up to you.

# Hokkaido soup curry

People from all over Japan travel to Hokkaido for this dish. It is a light but warming curried soup, but the real heart of the dish is the way it shows off Hokkaido's reputation for excellent produce. You don't need to get your vegetables sent from Japan to make it, but use the best quality you can find. It's worth it.

**Serves** / 4
**Prep** / 15 minutes **Cook** / 40 minutes

½ cup Garlic Oil (page 23) or 4 cloves garlic, peeled, chopped and fried in ½ cup vegetable oil

1 brown onion, peeled and finely sliced

500g pork mince

¼ cup fish sauce

¼ cup soy sauce

¼ cup water

1 tsp caster sugar

1kg fresh thin egg noodles, or equivalent quantity dried flat noodles or fettuccine

4 spring onions, trimmed and white and light green part finely sliced, to serve

## PICKLED GREEN CHILLIES

½ cup white vinegar

1 cup water

2 tbsp caster sugar

1 tsp salt

1 cup sliced large green chillies

For the pickled green chillies, mix together the vinegar, water, sugar and salt in a saucepan and stir over medium heat until the sugar is dissolved. Heat until steaming (not boiling) and pour the warm liquid over the chillies in a jar or heatproof container. Allow to cool to room temperature and transfer to the fridge at least overnight, however the flavour will be better after 3–4 days.

Heat the Garlic Oil in a saucepan over medium heat and fry the onion until it starts to brown. Add the pork and fry until it is well browned. Add the fish sauce, soy sauce, sugar and water and stir well. Cook for a further minute. The mixture should be oily with a bit of flavourful liquid at the bottom. If you can't see any oil in the dish, add a bit more Garlic Oil.

Bring a large pot of water to the boil and blanch the noodles for 1 minute, or until softened and cooked through. If using dry noodles or fettuccine, cook according to the packet instructions. Divide the noodles or pasta between four bowls.

Place a large spoonful of the pork and its oily liquid over the noodles (the oil will act as a dressing), scatter with spring onions and serve with the pickled green chillies on the side.

TIP / If you want to add vegetables to this dish, a few blanched Asian greens are perfect. You don't need to add flavour to the greens separately, as they can also be dressed with the oily sauce from the pork.

# Hakka noodles

These noodles are very popular around where my uncle used to live in Seremban in Malaysia. Instead of being the main focus of the dish, the fried pork and garlic oil are just a dressing for the noodles, balanced by the bite of pickled chillies. Around Seremban this dish is made with flat wheat noodles, but many other types of noodle and pasta work just as well.

**Serves** / 4
**Prep** / 10 minutes  **Stand** / Overnight  **Cook** / 10 minutes

500ml Prawn Stock (page 18)
1 litre water
¼ cup Tom Yum Paste (page 23) or commercial paste
4 kaffir lime leaves (optional)
2 tomatoes, quartered
1 cup button mushrooms, quartered
1 red capsicum, deseeded and cut into 2cm × 5cm pieces
1 cup broccoli florets
16 raw prawns, peeled and deveined
2 tsp fish sauce, to serve
4 tsp freshly squeezed lime juice or lemon juice, to serve
1 cup fresh coriander leaves, to serve

Bring the Prawn Stock and water to the boil in a large pot and add the Tom Yum Paste and kaffir lime leaves (if using). Boil for 5 minutes, or until the broth is fragrant. Add the tomatoes, mushrooms and capsicum and simmer for 1 minute. Add the broccoli and prawns and simmer for a further 2 minutes, or until the prawns are cooked through.

In each of four separate bowls add ½ tsp of fish sauce and 1 tsp lime juice. Ladle the soup and ingredients into each bowl and scatter with coriander leaves.

**TIP** / For a bit of extra flavour and heat you can add a few spoons of Thai roasted red chilli paste (nam prik pao) to this dish if you like. It is available from Asian supermarkets.

# Tom yum soup

The Thai version of this simple but strongly flavoured soup is made by boiling together aromatics such as lemongrass and kaffir lime with prawns and mushrooms. To save time, I prefer to make a paste that keeps really well but still retains its fresh flavour. I also like to add extra vegetables to make it a more substantial light meal.

**Serves** / 4
**Prep** / 10 minutes **Cook** / 10 minutes

'It's incredible to think how many of the conversations we have with our loved ones take place across a table, and over a plate.'

6 chicken Marylands or a whole
    free-range chicken (1.8kg)
6 Steamed Eggs (page 228) or
    soft-boiled eggs, peeled
1½ litres water
1½ cups soy sauce
1½ cups dark soy sauce
1 brown onion, halved, skin on
5cm ginger, thickly sliced
2 star anise
2 cinnamon sticks
1 cup caster sugar
Coriander leaves and steamed rice,
    to serve

Add all the ingredients except the chicken and the eggs to a very large pot. Bring to the boil, stirring to dissolve the sugar.

Add the chicken pieces to the pot (add a little more water if necessary to completely cover the chicken) and return to a simmer. Simmer over medium heat for 35 minutes, or until the chicken is cooked through. Turn off the heat and allow the chicken to cool in the liquid for a further 15 minutes. Remove and discard the onion, ginger and spices. (If you aren't planning to eat the chicken straight away, allow it to sit in the poaching liquid for longer – even overnight in the fridge – as it will take on more colour and flavour.)

Remove the chicken from the poaching liquid and keep warm, covered, in the oven. Place the peeled eggs in a separate bowl and ladle over enough of the poaching liquid to cover them completely. A piece of baking paper or cling wrap will help to keep the eggs submerged.

Bring the pot back to the boil, uncovered, and reduce the volume by half. This will take about 15 minutes.

Serve the chicken with the halved eggs and drizzle with the reduced poaching liquid. Scatter with coriander and serve a little extra reduced liquid on the side. Serve with steamed rice.

TIP / The reduced poaching liquid is also a delicious dressing for steamed fish, eggs or tofu, and can even be diluted again to poach more soy sauce chicken. If you want to be a bit more adventurous, poaching in this stock is also a great way to cook liver.

# Soy sauce chicken

You can't get a much simpler dish than piling a bunch of ingredients into a pot and letting them cook together. The chicken and eggs take on great flavour from the poaching liquid, but instead of cooking the eggs together with the chicken I prefer to keep them separate so that the yolks stay soft.

**Serves** / 6
**Prep** / 10 minutes  **Cook** / 1 hour

50g unsalted butter
2 brown onions, peeled and coarsely
    grated
1 tbsp minced garlic
1 tbsp grated ginger
1 tsp turmeric
½ tsp chilli powder
½ tsp ground coriander
1 tsp ground cumin
½ tsp ground cinnamon
½ tsp salt
1 tbsp sugar
1 can (400g) diced tomatoes
1 full recipe portion Tandoori Chicken
    (page 191), cut into bite-sized pieces
150ml thickened cream
2 tbsp shredded coriander leaves,
    to serve
Steamed rice, to serve

Heat the butter over medium heat in a large saucepan (big enough to hold all the sauce ingredients plus the Tandoori Chicken). Add the onion, garlic and ginger and cook for about 5 minutes, stirring frequently. Add the turmeric, chilli, coriander, cumin, cinnamon, salt and sugar and stir for a further minute, or until the spices are fragrant. Add the tomatoes plus 200ml water (just half-fill the can with water and pour it into the pot). Bring to the boil and reduce the heat to a simmer. Simmer for 15 minutes, stirring occasionally, then blend the sauce with a stick blender until smooth.

Stir the chicken pieces and cream into the sauce. Return to a simmer and turn off the heat. Adjust for seasoning with a little salt if necessary. Scatter the butter chicken with shredded coriander and serve with rice.

TIP / If you don't have time to make Tandoori Chicken for this dish you can quickly chargrill or pan-fry some chicken thighs, slice them and simmer them in the smooth, blended sauce for an extra 5 minutes to cook through completely.

# Butter chicken

**Murgh makhani** / Is there a more loved Indian dish around the world than butter chicken? A good butter chicken will always start with Tandoori Chicken (page 191). It might be a slight inconvenience, but the extra time taken to roast or grill the chicken gives this dish the savoury earthiness needed to balance the sweet, creamy butter sauce.

**Serves** / 6
**Prep** / 15 minutes  **Cook** / 30 minutes

1 whole free-range chicken
    (about 1.8kg)
3 cups Shaoxing wine
¼ cup caster sugar
1 tbsp salt
5cm ginger, sliced and bruised with
    the flat of a knife
2 spring onions, trimmed
1 litre water
Steamed rice, to serve

Wash the chicken under running water, including inside the cavity, and drain well.

Place the wine, sugar, salt, ginger and spring onion in a large pot with the water and bring to the boil. Add the chicken breast-side down and return to a low simmer. Add more water to keep the chicken completely submerged if necessary. Simmer, covered, for 35 minutes, then turn off the heat and allow the chicken to stand in the simmering liquid for about 1 hour while the liquid cools.

Remove the chicken from the liquid and slice it into portions.

The chicken can be either chilled in the fridge and served cold, or at room temperature, or warm in a bowl with a bit of the poaching liquid. Serve with steamed rice. This matches well with some Pickled Cabbage (page 220), Ajat (page 228) or Ginger-pickled Cucumber (page 224).

**TIP** / Many of the flavours in food are more soluble in alcohol than water. As well as the taste of the alcohol itself, cooking with alcohol as a seasoning will draw out and enhance the natural flavours of other ingredients.

# Drunken chicken

Alcohol is a vital ingredient in cooking, and I don't just mean a sneaky glass of wine while you're stirring. Adding a dash gives depth without needing a long list of ingredients, and this dish is a great example. With a few ingredients you can create a dish that's full of character. This is like a light, fresh Chinese coq au vin – perfect for summer.

**Serves** / 4
**Prep** / 10 minutes  **Cook** / 40 minutes  **Stand** / 1 hour

big
pan

2 tbsp vegetable oil
3 cloves garlic, peeled and sliced
2 good-quality sirloin steaks
   (about 300g each)
Steamed rice, to serve

**LIGHT TERIYAKI GLAZE**
3 tbsp soy sauce
2 tbsp sake
2 tbsp mirin
1 tbsp caster sugar

To make the teriyaki glaze mix together all the ingredients and stir to dissolve the sugar. If the sugar doesn't dissolve, heat the glaze in the microwave for 10–20 seconds, or in a small saucepan over low heat, and stir again until dissolved.

Heat a heavy frypan over medium heat and add the oil. Fry the garlic until lightly browned, then remove and drain on paper towel. Increase the heat to medium–high and add the steaks, browning each steak well on both sides.

Add the glaze to the pan around the steaks and repeatedly flip the steaks through the glaze. Cook the steaks to your liking. As the glaze begins to thicken it will stick to the steaks. Remove the steaks to a warm plate in a draught-free place, pour over any sticky glaze left in the pan, and rest for 5 minutes.

Slice the steaks, arrange the slices on a plate and scatter over the fried garlic. Serve with rice and Ginger-pickled Cucumber (page 224).

**TIP** / Make a big batch of the teriyaki glaze. From chicken to fish, or even in a repeat performance of this dish, you'll find it indispensable. For enough to fill an old wine bottle use 250ml soy sauce, 200ml each of sake and mirin, and around 80g sugar.

# Teriyaki steak

The Japanese style of teriyaki is a sweet glaze often used to coat fish, meat or chicken. This more authentic style of teriyaki may look different to Westernised stir-fry versions, but if you use high-quality steak this easy, homemade glaze will produce a dish that's way ahead of the pack.

**Serves** / 4
**Prep** / 5 minutes  **Cook** / 10 minutes  **Rest** / 5 minutes

800g pork belly, skin and bones removed, sliced into long strips about 1cm thick
Salt and pepper, to taste
1 large onion, peeled and cut into thick slices (but not separated to rings)
2 cups kimchi, to serve
8 leaves Korean sesame leaf (perilla), to serve (optional)
1 head butter lettuce, to serve
1 large green chilli, sliced, to serve
3 cloves garlic, peeled and thinly sliced, to serve

**SALTED SESAME OIL**
2 tbsp sesame oil
½ tsp salt flakes

**SOY SAUCE & VINEGAR**
2 tbsp soy sauce
1 tbsp rice vinegar
A pinch of caster sugar
½ tsp toasted sesame seeds, lightly crushed

**SSAMJANG**
3 tbsp white miso (or doenjang, Korean fermented soy bean paste)
2 tbsp gochujang (Korean chilli bean paste)
2 tbsp rice vinegar
2 tbsp mirin
1 tbsp sesame oil
2 tsp Garlic Paste (page 23) or 2 cloves garlic, peeled and minced
¼ cup grated onion
2 spring onions, trimmed and finely chopped
1 tsp honey
1 tsp caster sugar

Lightly season the pork with salt and pepper and grill until well browned on a hot, oiled barbecue with the onion slices, making sure the onion slices soak up some of the fat from the pork. Cut the pork into short lengths with a pair of kitchen scissors.

For each of the dipping sauces, mix the ingredients together until combined.

Serve the pork with the fresh ingredients and the condiments. Dip the pork into the sauce of your choice, wrap it in a lettuce leaf with a little kimchi and any other ingredients you like, and enjoy.

TIP / This is the perfect barbecue dish for a crowd. Bring out all the condiments and wraps, and then just grill the pork on the barbecue and you're done.

# Korean grilled pork belly

**Samgyeopsal** / Pork belly is an extremely versatile cut – it doesn't need to be slow braised or roasted with crispy skin every time you have it (but don't let me stop you!). One of my favourite ways to cook it is Korean barbecue style – grilled and served with lettuce, kimchi and a few easy condiments. Included here is ssamjang, a classic Korean sauce.

**Serves** / 4
**Prep** / 25 minutes  **Cook** / 10 minutes

1 tbsp vegetable oil

4 large chicken thigh fillets, cut into 5cm pieces

1 large onion, peeled, halved and cut into 1cm slices

2 cups Whole Chicken Stock (page 18)

¼ cup soy sauce

¼ cup sake

¼ cup mirin

¼ tsp salt

1 tbsp caster sugar

8 free-range eggs, yolks broken and very lightly whisked

8 cups warm cooked short-grain rice, to serve

1 sheet nori, finely sliced

2 spring onions, trimmed and finely sliced, to serve

Heat the oil in a large frypan over medium heat. Fry the chicken pieces until just lightly browned then stir through the onion. Add the chicken stock, soy sauce, sake, mirin, salt and sugar and bring to a simmer. Simmer for 3–4 minutes, or until the chicken is nearly cooked through and the onion is softened. Reduce the heat to low.

Pour over the whisked eggs and stir once. You should still be able to see areas of white and yolk separated in the egg. Allow the eggs to barely set softly and remove the pan from the heat. Sit the base of the pan on a tea towel soaked in cold water to draw the heat from the pan and stop the eggs from overcooking.

Divide the warm cooked rice between four bowls. Scatter the rice with the nori and spoon over a portion of the chicken and egg mixture (enough to cover the rice completely).

Scatter the top of the egg with spring onion. This is great served with Ginger-pickled Cucumber (page 224) and Basic Miso Soup (page 225) on the side.

TIP / Once you've mastered the 'parent and child rice bowl' try a 'tanindon' or 'stranger rice bowl'. It's the same process, but instead of matching egg with the familiar chicken, the chicken is replaced with a stranger – thinly sliced pork.

# Big pan oyakodon

'Oyako' in Japanese means 'parent and child', with reference to the chicken and egg used in this dish, and 'don' is short for donburi – a rice bowl. Teriyaki chicken may be popular overseas but in Japan, the oyakodon is the go-to chicken dish for family comfort food.

**Serves** / 4
**Prep** / 10 minutes  **Cook** / 10 minutes

600g chicken thigh fillets
1 tbsp cornflour
2 tbsp Garlic Oil (page 23) or
    vegetable oil
1 brown onion, peeled, halved and
    thinly sliced
1 green capsicum, deseeded and cut
    into 5cm × 2cm pieces
2 tbsp Garlic Paste (page 23) or
    6 cloves garlic, peeled and crushed
3 tbsp white miso
2 tbsp sake
2 tbsp mirin
Steamed rice, to serve

Slice the chicken thigh fillets in half lengthways then slice each half diagonally into medallions. Toss in a little cornflour and set aside.

Heat a large frypan over high heat and add the Garlic Oil. Add the chicken and toss in the pan until browned (you may need to do this in batches). Add the onion and capsicum and toss until the capsicum is just softened.

Mix together the Garlic Paste, miso, sake and mirin and pour it into the pan, tossing to make sure the chicken and vegetables are well coated. Toss in the pan for 2–3 minutes, or until the miso is toasted and fragrant and the sauce is thickened. Remove from the heat and set aside to rest for 2 minutes before serving with steamed rice.

TIP / Always add something sweet when using miso or soy sauce for marinating, grilling or stir-frying. The sweetness of mirin, honey or sugar balances the strongly savoury flavour of the miso or soy sauce brought out by the heat.

# Garlic miso chicken

Miso isn't just an ingredient used for soups – its umami flavour makes it perfect for grilling or even stir-frying, and it's a great addition to meat marinades. As the miso cooks it produces a toasted, savoury aroma.

**Serves** / 4
**Prep** / 10 minutes  **Cook** / 10 minutes

16 large raw prawns, peeled and
    deveined
2 cups broccoli florets
3 tbsp Garlic Oil (page 23)
1 tsp salt flakes
1 tbsp Garlic Paste (page 23)
½ cup spring onions, trimmed and
    cut into 5cm lengths
1 tbsp Shaoxing wine
3 tbsp Whole Chicken Stock (page 18)
    or water
1 tsp rice vinegar
A pinch of caster sugar
1 tsp cornflour, mixed with 2 tbsp
    cold water
Coriander leaves and steamed rice,
    to serve

Butterfly the prawns by cutting through their backs almost the entire way and pressing them with the flat of your knife. Blanch the broccoli florets in salted water for 30 seconds and drain well, or microwave them sprinkled with water and covered for 1 minute.

Heat the oil in a wok over high heat and add the prawns. Toss to coat in the oil and season with the salt. Add in the Garlic Paste and toss for about a minute. Add in the broccoli and spring onions and continue to toss for a further minute. Add the Shaoxing wine, chicken stock or water, rice vinegar and sugar and toss well to combine. Slowly add the cornflour mixture while tossing the pan until the sauce thickens. Scatter the prawns and broccoli with coriander and serve with rice.

**TIP** / Spending a few minutes butterflying the prawns in this way does wonders for the final texture of this dish. The butterflied prawns are succulent and crisp. It's a bit of extra effort, but try it once and you'll see why it's worth it. For a variation on this dish, try substituting the broccoli with green garlic shoots or asparagus.

# Garlic prawns
# & broccoli

When we were growing up my sister's two favourite foods were garlic prawns and broccoli. It's no coincidence that they go fantastically together. This is a great way to make use of your Garlic Oil and Garlic Paste (page 23), but if you don't have any at hand, just begin this dish by frying four cloves of crushed garlic in three tablespoons of oil.

**Serves** / 4
**Prep** / 15 minutes  **Cook** / 5 minutes

- 600g rump steak
- 2 tbsp oyster sauce
- 1 tbsp fish sauce
- 1 tbsp sugar
- 1 tsp sesame oil
- 1 tbsp peanut oil
- 3 cloves garlic, peeled and roughly chopped
- Freshly ground black pepper, to taste
- Butter lettuce leaves, to serve
- 1 red onion, peeled and thinly sliced, to serve
- 1 tomato, thinly sliced, to serve
- Lemon wedges, to serve
- Freshly ground salt and black pepper, to taste
- Steamed rice, to serve (optional)

Cut the rump steak into 3cm cubes and trim any fatty pieces (although I don't mind keeping a bit of fat on for a more indulgent texture). Mix the beef with the oyster sauce, fish sauce, sugar and sesame oil. Set aside to marinate for 10 minutes.

Heat the peanut oil in a large frypan (preferably non-stick) until very hot and smoking. Spread the beef out over the pan in a single layer with a bit of space between each cube. Fry without stirring for about 1 minute, or until the marinade caramelises on the outside of the beef and it is well browned on the surface touching the pan. Now shake the pan well to flip the beef and using tongs, turn any pieces of the beef if necessary so that the browned side is facing up. Scatter the garlic over the top of the beef and cook for a further minute. Shake the pan again and cook for a further 30 seconds then remove the beef from the pan. The beef should be well caramelised and browned. Grind over plenty of black pepper.

To serve, arrange the lettuce, onion and tomato on a platter, squeeze over some lemon juice and season with salt and grind over some black pepper. Place the shaking beef on the vegetables and serve on its own or with rice.

TIP / In the unlikely event that there are any leftovers from this dish, the beef and salad vegetables make a fantastic sandwich in a warm, buttered baguette.

# Shaking beef

**Bo luc lac** / 'Shaking beef' is a direct translation of the Vietnamese name for this dish and comes from the process of shaking the pan to toss the cubes of beef. It's often done in a wok, but I prefer to cook it in a very large frypan because the flat pan's uniform heat makes it easier to spread out the cubes and increase the surface area for faster browning.

**Serves** / 4
**Prep** / 10 minutes  **Marinate** / 10 minutes  **Cook** / 10 minutes

3 tbsp vegetable oil
8 raw prawns, peeled and deveined
200g squid, scored and cut into
　　bite-sized pieces
2 cloves garlic, peeled and roughly
　　chopped
1 small brown onion, peeled and sliced
2 cups shredded cabbage
1 small carrot, sliced into fine
　　matchsticks
1kg fresh udon noodles
2 cups bean sprouts
2 tbsp aonori flakes, to serve (optional)
¼ cup loosely packed bonito flakes,
　　to serve (optional)
Red Radish Pickles (page 224), to
　　serve (optional)

**YAKISOBA SAUCE**
2 tbsp soy sauce
2 tbsp dark soy sauce
2 tbsp oyster sauce
2 tbsp mirin
2 tsp caster sugar

To make the yakisoba sauce, mix together the ingredients in a small bowl and stir until the sugar is dissolved. A little sugar remaining undissolved is fine.

Heat the barbecue hotplate until very hot and add about half of the vegetable oil. Fry the prawns and squid, moving them constantly with spatulas until they are half cooked. Add the garlic, onion, cabbage and carrot and continue to cook, adding more oil as necessary, until the vegetables start to soften.

Add the udon noodles, the remaining oil and the yakisoba sauce and fry everything together for 3 minutes, or until the noodles are soft and cooked through. Add the bean sprouts and toss for about 30 seconds, or until softened.

Scatter with the aonori, bonito flakes and Red Radish Pickles (if using) and serve.

**TIP** / For a variation, try these noodles with pork belly slices or pieces of chicken along with the seafood. Aonori flakes are different from the sheets of nori seaweed used for wrapping sushi. They are available from Japanese grocers but you can substitute nori sheets processed to fine flakes in a food processor.

# Barbecue
# noodles

Fried noodles may not seem like the most natural barbecue dish, but don't tell that to the Japanese – a barbecue hotplate makes a great home teppanyaki grill. Fried udon noodles or egg noodles are a must at any Japanese barbecue, and a great way to use the barbecue for a family dinner. Use a couple of spatulas to keep the food moving and you'll get great results.

**Serves** / 4
**Prep** / 15 minutes  **Cook** / 10 minutes

1 block (300g) firm tofu, drained
500g beef mince
1 onion, peeled and coarsely grated
1 egg
½ tsp salt
¼ tsp nutmeg
2 tbsp vegetable oil
¼ cup water
¼ daikon radish, finely grated, to serve
2 spring onions, finely sliced, to serve
Steamed rice, to serve

**PONZU**
1 tbsp sake
2 tbsp mirin
¼ cup soy sauce
A pinch of caster sugar
2 tbsp lemon juice

Turn the tofu out onto a double layer of paper towel, wrap it, then put a heavy plate on top and let it stand for about 20 minutes to press out any excess water. Break apart the tofu and mix it together with the beef mince, grated onion, egg, salt and nutmeg. Refrigerate for 30 minutes then form into four thick oval patties.

To make the ponzu, place the sake and mirin in a small saucepan over medium heat and bring to the boil. Remove from the heat and add the soy sauce, sugar and lemon juice and allow to cool.

Heat the oil in a large frypan over medium heat, add the hamburger patties and fry for about 3 minutes, or until well browned on one side. Flip and fry for a further minute, then add the water to the pan and cover. Allow the patties to steam for 2–3 minutes, or until they are cooked through.

Squeeze out any excess moisture from the radish. Top each Hamburg with a large spoon of grated radish, scatter with the spring onions and pour over the ponzu. Serve with steamed rice.

**TIP** / Instead of the grated daikon and ponzu, you could also serve these Tofu Hamburgs with some steamed vegetables and any of your favourite steak accompaniments like demi-glace or sautéed mushrooms, or substitute the water with about a cup of red wine that you can reduce to make a simple red wine pan jus.

# Tofu Hamburg

In Japan, a Hamburg steak is even more popular than the classic hamburger. While the sandwich-style American favourite is served in a bun, the Hamburg steak is a patty of minced beef served on its own, often with rice and vegetables. The Japanese love the fluffy texture created by mixing the beef with tofu instead of breadcrumbs.

**Serves** / 4
**Prep** / 25 minutes **Refrigerate** / 30 minutes **Cook** / 10 minutes

1 tbsp vegetable oil
500g chicken mince
¼ cup soy sauce
¼ cup sake
2 tbsp caster sugar
2 tbsp mirin
¼ cup water
2 cups snow peas, tailed
8 cups steamed short-grain rice,
    to serve
1 sheet nori, finely sliced, to serve

**EGG CRUMBLE**
4 eggs
2 tbsp mirin
1 tsp caster sugar
½ tsp salt

Heat the oil in a medium saucepan over medium heat and add the chicken mince. Fry the mince until it turns white (you don't need to brown it) and add the soy sauce, sake, sugar, mirin and water. Bring to a simmer, stirring occasionally for about 10 minutes, or until the liquid has almost completely evaporated. Stir again to moisten the chicken and set aside.

To make the egg crumble, heat the eggs, mirin, sugar and salt together in a medium saucepan over medium heat, stirring frequently for about 10 minutes, or until the egg dries and is in small pieces.

Blanch the snow peas in boiling salted water for about 1 minute, then refresh in cold water. Cut the snow peas in half diagonally.

Divide the rice between four bowls and press down to create a flat surface. Arrange the chicken, sliced snow peas and egg crumble in sections over the top of the rice. Serve with sliced nori.

TIP / This recipe works equally well with pork, turkey or beef mince. For the snow peas you could substitute cooked green peas, or blanched green beans sliced into rounds.

# Chicken soboro

This simple one-bowl dish is loved by adults and kids alike. Although the egg crumble may look like dry scrambled eggs, it is the perfect texture to match with soft white short-grain rice, moist chicken and fresh snow peas.

**Serves** / 4
**Prep** / 10 minutes  **Cook** / 20 minutes

3 small zucchini, trimmed
½ tsp salt
1 small onion, peeled and sliced
1 cup plain flour
2 tbsp potato flour or cornflour
2 eggs
1 tbsp sesame oil
2 tbsp vegetable oil

**DIPPING SAUCE**
2 tbsp light soy sauce
1 tbsp rice vinegar
1 tsp sesame oil
¼ tsp chilli powder
A pinch of sugar

Slice the zucchini into matchsticks without waste by first slicing them on a steep diagonal, then stack up the diagonal slices and slice those into matchsticks. Place the matchsticks in a bowl and scatter with the salt, tossing through the zucchini to make sure it is well distributed. Leave the zucchini for about 10 minutes, or until it softens. Lightly squeeze the zucchini to extract the liquid, reserving it in a small bowl.

Stir the onion slices through the zucchini and add the flours and eggs and mix well. Loosen the batter by adding about ⅓ cup of the reserved zucchini liquid. Don't stir the batter too much or your pancakes may be tough – a few lumps is fine.

For the dipping sauce, mix together all the ingredients until the sugar is dissolved.

Heat a large frypan over high heat and add the oils. Add large tablespoons of the zucchini mixture to the pan, flattening them out to 10cm patties. Fry for about 3 minutes on each side, or until golden brown. Serve the pancakes immediately with the dipping sauce.

TIP / Once you have the basic technique and batter mix for these pancakes, you can make them with just about any meat, seafood or vegetable. Try them with chopped kimchi (including the kimchi juice) for another Korean favourite.

# Korean zucchini pancakes

**Hobak buchimgae /** These versatile Korean pancakes work well with zucchini but once you have the technique down, you can vary the ingredients to suit whatever you have in the fridge: mixed vegetables, seafood, even thinly sliced meats. The world is your pancake!

**Serves** / 4
**Prep** / 15 minutes  **Stand** / 10 minutes  **Cook** / 15 minutes

1 tbsp olive oil
600g whiting fillets
Salt, to season
4 tbsp Nori Butter (page 17), softened
    to room temperature

Heat a heavy frypan or barbecue and brush it with olive oil. Season the fish fillets with salt and fry skin-side down first for about 2 minutes on each side, or until the fish is barely cooked through. Brush with the softened Nori Butter throughout the cooking process. Rest the fish for a minute or two to complete cooking.

Brush with a little more Nori Butter to serve.

TIP / I prefer to use King George whiting for this dish, but you can substitute any white fish. Alternatively, you can use the butter to flavour grilled chicken fillets.

# Whiting with nori butter

Having some nori butter in the fridge can mean dinner in less than 10 minutes. Anyone who says they don't have time to cook needs to give this a go. This is a perfect light meal when teamed with a crisp green salad, steamed rice or boiled potatoes.

**Serves** / 4
**Prep** / 2 minutes  **Cook** / 5 minutes

1 tbsp vegetable oil

2 good-quality sirloin steaks (about 300g each), at room temperature

Salt, to season

1 bunch asparagus (8–10 spears), trimmed and halved

8 cups steamed rice, to serve

1 sheet nori, cut into quarters

2 tbsp Nori Butter (page 17), softened

Red Radish Pickles (page 224), to serve

Heat a heavy frypan or grill pan over high heat and brush with a little oil. Season the steaks well with salt and grill them until cooked to your liking. Rest in a draught-free place for about 5 minutes.

While the steaks are resting, grill the asparagus for about 3 minutes, turning frequently until just cooked.

Divide the rice between four bowls and top each bowl with a square of nori. Cut the steaks into thick slices and divide the steak and asparagus between the bowls. Brush the steak slices and asparagus liberally with the Nori Butter and serve some Red Radish Pickles on the side.

**TIP** / When it comes to steak, there is no substitute for quality. I prefer to buy the best-quality meat I can afford to enjoy in smaller quantities rather than buying cheap steaks that are big, but tough and flavourless.

# Steak & asparagus donburi

This simple rice bowl dish is a great way to enjoy good steak, and you don't need a whole big slab to yourself. The Nori Butter melts over everything to add extra flavour to the steak and asparagus, as well as lightly oiling the rice.

**Serves** / 4
**Prep** / 5 minutes  **Cook** / 10 minutes  **Rest** / 5 minutes

4 chicken thigh fillets, skin on
   (about 800g)
½ cup potato flour or cornflour
About 1 litre canola oil, for shallow-
   frying
2 cups shredded iceberg lettuce,
   to serve

**YURINCHI SAUCE**
3 tbsp rice vinegar
2 tbsp caster sugar
2 tbsp soy sauce
3 large spring onions, trimmed and
   finely chopped
1 tbsp toasted sesame seeds
1 tsp sesame oil
1 clove garlic, peeled and minced
½ tsp grated ginger

Lightly coat the chicken in the potato flour and set aside, uncovered, for about 5 minutes. Heat the oil in a deep frypan to 180°C and shallow-fry the chicken thighs, one or two at a time, for about 3 minutes on each side, or until golden brown and cooked through. Keep the cooked thighs warm on a wire rack in a low oven while you cook the remaining chicken.

For the yurinchi sauce, mix together all the ingredients in a non-reactive bowl until the sugar dissolves.

Arrange the shredded lettuce on a large plate. Slice the chicken thighs into 2cm slices and place on the shredded lettuce. Pour over the yurinchi sauce and serve immediately.

TIP / For light and crisp results when shallow-frying or deep-frying a good rule of thumb is that what you are frying should not cover more than half of the surface area of the pan. Overloading the pan causes the oil temperature to drop too much, resulting in soggy, oily food.

# Yurinchi

This Japanese interpretation of Chinese 'oil-drenched chicken' (yóulínjī) may be the precursor to dishes such as lemon chicken that have found their way all over the world. Featuring fried chicken with a light sweet–sour vinegar sauce, yurinchi is surprisingly light and fresh. It's one of my absolute favourites.

**Serves** / 4
**Prep** / 15 minutes  **Cook** / 15 minutes

½ cup vegetable oil

4 chicken thigh fillets (about 600g), skin removed and sliced into bite-sized pieces

1 brown onion, peeled and finely chopped

1 cup frozen peas

2 cups sliced button mushrooms

8 cups cooked short-grain rice

½ tsp salt

¼ cup soy sauce

4 tbsp tomato sauce

Salt and white pepper

8 eggs, beaten

¼ cup finely chopped chives, to serve

Heat half the vegetable oil in a wok or large frypan over high heat. Add the chicken and fry until lightly browned. Add the onion, peas and mushrooms and toss until the mushrooms are softened. Add the rice, salt, soy sauce and tomato sauce and toss for about 5 minutes, or until the rice is coated and the sauces are fragrant. Season with salt, add a pinch of white pepper and turn out onto a large platter, moulding the mound of rice into the shape of a rugby ball.

Heat a large frypan the same size as your serving platter over medium heat, and add the remaining oil, ensuring the pan is completely covered. Add the beaten egg and with a few long strokes draw the cooked egg away from the edges of the pan, allowing the raw egg to fill the gaps as if making an omelette.

As the bottom of the omelette cooks (but the top is still raw), fold the two sides of the omelette into the centre to form a folded omelette with a seam down the centre.

Place the folded omelette on top of the mound of rice with the seam facing up. Break the seam carefully with your fingers, allowing the omelette to flow down and wrap the rice. Scatter with the chives and serve.

TIP / Don't let the difficulty in making a soft omelette scare you off this dish. It's delicious no matter how the omelette is cooked. Even leaving out the omelette altogether, this dish is known in Japan simply as 'chicken rice'. It's a favourite among adults and children alike.

# Omuraisu

Japanese 'omuraisu' (omelette rice) has to be one of my favourite comfort foods. It borrows a little from China, a little from Southeast Asia and a little from the West for a dish that is completely Japanese. The key to a great omuraisu is the velvety, half-cooked soft omelette that wraps the rice. Just perfect.

**Serves** / 4
**Prep** / 20 minutes  **Cook** / 20 minutes

big
dish

1 whole free-range chicken
    (about 1.8kg)
1 tbsp curry powder
1 tsp turmeric
½ tsp chilli powder (optional)
75g butter, melted
1 lemon, cut into eighths
1 red onion, peeled and cut into eighths
2 tbsp yoghurt
1 tsp honey

Heat the oven to 180°C (fan-forced). With kitchen scissors or a heavy knife, cut the backbone out of the chicken and press down on the breast to flatten it. Mix together the curry powder, turmeric, chilli powder (if using) and melted butter and let stand for 10 minutes. Melt the butter again if necessary and brush all over the chicken, inside, outside and under the skin.

Place the lemon and red onion in a pile on a roasting tray and place the chicken on top. Roast for 45 minutes, basting occasionally with any pan juices. Remove the chicken from the oven and switch the oven to the overhead grill setting, set to maximum heat.

Mix together the yoghurt and honey and drizzle over the skin of the chicken. A squeeze bottle is perfect for this. Return the chicken to the oven and grill for 10 minutes, or until the yoghurt and honey mix is dark and caramelised. Rest for 20 minutes in a warm, draught-free place before serving. This chicken is great with some Ajat (page 228) and/or Tomato Salad (page 227) on the side.

TIP / The importance of resting meats after cooking isn't just limited to steaks. Even big cuts of roast meat and whole chickens will benefit from a long rest between cooking and serving to allow the juices to redistribute themselves within the meat.

# Tiger-skin chicken

This variation on a roast chicken is an easy family dinner that's a hit with kids. The dark stripes of grilled yoghurt and honey are both delicious and a bit of fun.

**Serves** / 4
**Prep** / 25 minutes  **Cook** / 55 minutes  **Rest** / 20 minutes

4 leaves Chinese cabbage
1 whole snapper (about 1kg), cleaned and scaled
3 spring onions, roots removed
2 tbsp soy sauce
2 tbsp Shaoxing wine
½ tsp salt
1 tsp caster sugar
5cm ginger, peeled and cut into thin matchsticks
2 tbsp vegetable oil
Coriander leaves, to serve

Heat the oven to 220°C. Lay out a double layer of aluminium foil on a large baking tray with enough foil to completely wrap around the fish. Place 2 leaves of Chinese cabbage on the foil and place the fish on top.

Cut diagonal slits to the bone about 5cm apart on both sides of the fish. Trim the dark green tops from the spring onions and place them in the cavity of the fish. Finely slice the remainder of the spring onion and set aside in the fridge.

Mix together the soy sauce, Shaoxing wine, salt and sugar and stir to dissolve. Pour the mixture over the fish and into the cavity. Scatter the top of the fish with the ginger. Cover the fish with 2 more leaves of Chinese cabbage and fold over the aluminium foil to completely encase the fish.

Place the fish in the oven for 30 minutes then remove and carefully open the aluminium foil, making sure not to lose any of the juices inside. Discard the spring onion tops and Chinese cabbage (or you can serve the fish with the cabbage if you prefer). Transfer the fish to a large plate together with all the collected juices. Scatter the fish with the reserved sliced spring onion. Heat the oil in a separate pan until smoking and pour over the fish, spring onion and ginger. Scatter with coriander leaves and serve.

**TIP** / Although baking is the best alternative to steaming for this fish dish, it would be remiss of me not to tell you that many Asian families cook whole fish like this in the microwave. You can do away with the Chinese cabbage and foil and just microwave the fish and seasonings covered with cling wrap for about 6–8 minutes depending on the size of the fish, then finish the fish with the spring onion, oil and coriander as above.

# Oven-steamed snapper with ginger & spring onion

A Chinese-style steamed fish makes a quick and healthy dinner, but the challenge is usually to find a steamer big enough to fit a family-sized fish. This oven-steamed version of a classic Chinese dish gives you perfect results without needing to track down a giant steamer.

**Serves** / 6
**Prep** / 10 minutes  **Cook** / 30 minutes

1 whole free-range chicken
(about 1.8kg) or 2kg chicken wings
1 tbsp black peppercorns
Leaves, roots and stems from
2 coriander roots, roughly chopped
1 stalk lemongrass, white part only,
roughly chopped (optional)
2 tbsp brown sugar
¼ cup fish sauce
¼ cup coconut milk
Sweet Chilli Sauce (page 22), to serve

Halve the chickens with a cleaver through the backbone and breast cartilage. In a mortar pound the peppercorns, coriander and lemongrass together to a rough paste. Mix the paste with the brown sugar, fish sauce and coconut milk then rub this loose paste all over the chicken and marinate for at least 30 minutes, but preferably overnight.

Barbecue method: Grill the chicken on a low barbecue, turning frequently for 30 minutes or until cooked through. Rest in a warm, draught-free place for 15 minutes before serving.

Oven method: Heat the oven to 200°C (fan-forced). Place the chicken halves on a baking tray with the skin facing up and bake for 40 minutes, or until cooked through and caramelised. Rest in a warm, draught-free place for 15 minutes before serving. Grill under the overhead grill for a further 10 minutes if the chicken needs a little more colour.

Serve the chicken with Sweet Chilli Sauce.

TIP / The same marinade can also be used for boneless chicken thigh fillets, and it's fantastic when used as a rub for wings cooked on the barbecue.

# Thai grilled chicken

**Gai yang** / I've eaten so much good food in Thailand over the years that it's impossible to settle on just one stand-out dish. There is, however, one meal I'll never forget, and that's sitting out on a hot Bangkok night with a big group of friends, some bottles of Singha, and a seemingly endless quantity of exquisitely flavoured whole chickens, grilled over hot coals and served with real sweet chilli sauce. That memory always brings a smile to my face. It's an atmosphere I try to re-create myself at home every time I have a barbecue.

**Serves** / 4
**Prep** / 15 minutes  **Marinate** / 30 minutes  **Cook** / 40 minutes  **Rest** / 15 minutes

'Every dish we know began as something we cooked for the first time. It was only after we began to love them that they started to get that little bit easier.'

- 500g firm white-fleshed fish (basa, snapper or ling)
- 2 tbsp Easy Red Curry Paste (page 24) or commercial paste
- 2 tbsp fish sauce
- ½ tsp caster sugar
- 2 tbsp coconut cream (optional)
- 2 kaffir lime leaves, central vein removed and leaf very finely sliced
- 2 spring onions, trimmed and finely chopped
- 1 long red chilli, finely chopped
- 6 green beans, trimmed and cut into 1cm pieces
- 1 coriander root, root and stems finely chopped, leaves reserved
- 1 tbsp vegetable oil (if baking, or more if frying)
- Coriander leaves, to serve
- Ajat (page 228) and Sweet Chilli Sauce (page 22), to serve

Cut about a quarter of the fish into 2cm pieces and finely mince the remainder by chopping on a board. Add the red curry paste, fish sauce, sugar and coconut cream (if using) and continue to chop on the board with the fish until it is well mixed and resembles a thick paste.

Fold through the larger fish pieces, kaffir lime leaves, spring onions, chilli, beans and coriander and set aside until ready to cook.

Baking method: Heat the overhead grill in the oven to medium-hot. Form four large patties of the fish cake mixture on a tray lined with baking paper. Drizzle the patties with a little oil and grill for 8 minutes without turning until the patties are cooked through and lightly browned on top. Remove the patties from the paper with a spatula.

Deep-frying method: Heat a large saucepan or wok of oil to 180°C. Deep-fry tablespoons of the mixture for 2 minutes, or until golden brown.

Serve the fish cakes scattered with the coriander leaves and with some Ajat (page 228) or Sweet Chilli Sauce (page 22) on the side.

TIP / You can even pan-fry these fish cakes like hamburgers if you prefer. If frying, use a little more oil than you might think you need, as the fish cakes themselves are very lean.

# Baked Thai fish cakes

Fish cakes are a Thai snack that also make a great light meal. They are traditionally deep-fried, but if you keep the mix quite firm they can be baked with excellent results. I prefer to keep bigger chunks of fish in the mix for extra texture, which also means you don't have to drag out the food processor (or clean it later).

**Serves** / 4
**Prep** / 10 minutes **Cook** / 10 minutes

½ Kent pumpkin, seeds removed and sliced into wedges
3 tbsp fish sauce
1½ tbsp brown sugar
1 long red chilli, finely chopped
2 cloves garlic, peeled and finely chopped
2 tbsp vegetable oil
½ tsp salt flakes
½ cup thick Greek-style yoghurt
Lime wedges, to serve
Coriander leaves, to serve
Freshly ground black pepper, to taste

Heat the oven to 200°C (fan-forced). Place the pumpkin slices on a baking tray lined with baking paper. Mix together the fish sauce, brown sugar, chilli, garlic and oil and pour over the pumpkin, turning it over to coat well. Bake for 30 minutes without turning, or until the pumpkin is very well caramelised.

Scatter the pumpkin with salt and serve with spoonfuls of yoghurt, lime wedges and coriander leaves. Grind over black pepper to serve.

TIP / You don't need to peel pumpkin. The skin softens when cooked and provides a great texture. Just clean any dirt from the skin before slicing.

# Roasted pumpkin with coriander

Roasted pumpkin sits just on the border between sweet and savoury, and it can easily go either way. Chilli, garlic and fish sauce help this dish over the savoury line but you really need to caramelise the pumpkin well to remove some of the sweetness of the added sugar and balance the dish.

**Serves** / 4
**Prep** / 10 minutes  **Cook** / 30 minutes

½ cup thick yoghurt
1 tsp ground turmeric
2 tsp ground coriander
1 tsp salt
4 ling fillets, about 180g each
    (or snapper or blue-eye trevalla)
6 cups steamed rice, to serve
Lemon wedges, to serve

## GARLIC & GINGER SPINACH
1 tbsp Garlic Oil (page 23)
2cm ginger, peeled and cut into
    fine matchsticks
150g baby spinach leaves
Salt, to season

Mix together the yoghurt, turmeric and coriander and leave for 15 minutes for the colour and flavour to develop. Mix the salt through the yoghurt mixture and spread all over the fish fillets, with an especially thick layer on top. Place the fish on a baking tray lined with baking paper.

Heat the overhead grill in the oven to very hot. Grill the fish for 5–7 minutes, without turning, or until the yoghurt is browned and the fish is cooked through.

For the garlic and ginger spinach, heat the Garlic Oil in a wok over medium heat and add the ginger, frying for about 30 seconds until it is fragrant and lightly toasted. Add the spinach, season well with plenty of salt and toss until the spinach is wilted.

Divide the rice across four bowls and place the cooked spinach on top of each bowl then the fish on top of the spinach. Serve with lemon wedges.

**TIP** / I prefer a 50:50 mix of white and brown rice with this dish. The nuttiness of the brown rice really complements the fish. For a barbecue, you can cut the fish into large pieces for coating with the yoghurt mixture, then thread them onto skewers for grilling. Add a tablespoon of tandoori paste to the turmeric yoghurt if you want a stronger flavour.

# Grilled fish with turmeric yoghurt

My mother used to cook this simple fish dish as a healthy alternative for herself while we kids were devouring lamb chops and the like. I thought she was missing out until I first asked her if I could try the fish instead of what everyone else was eating. From that moment, I was hooked.

**Serves** / 4
**Prep** / 5 minutes **Wait** / 15 minutes **Cook** / 10 minutes

1 whole free-range chicken
   (about 1.8kg)
½ cup Nori Butter (page 17)
½ tsp salt
1 brown onion, peeled and cut
   into eighths

Heat the oven to 200°C (fan-forced).
Rinse the chicken under running water
and pat dry with paper towel. With your
fingers loosen the skin of the chicken
away from the meat. Push some of the
Nori Butter under the skin of the chicken
and brush the rest all over the skin.
Season with salt.

Place the onion wedges in a baking
dish and place the chicken on top.
Roast for 1 hour and 10 minutes, or
until the chicken is cooked through,
basting regularly with any pan juices.
Rest the chicken for 15 minutes in a
warm, draught-free place and serve.
This is great with some Japanese
Pumpkin Salad (page 225) and some
steamed green vegetables.

TIP / If you want to add some
vegetables around the chicken, a mix
of parboiled root vegetables such
as potato, carrot, daikon radish and
parsnip all cut into 5cm pieces, tossed
in olive oil and seasoned well with salt
will crisp in about the same time it takes
to cook the chicken.

# Nori butter
# roast chicken

Never underestimate the appeal of a simple roast chicken. But even
with your old favourites, it's good to give them a bit of a shake-up once
in a while. With a little pre-made Nori Butter, trying something new
doesn't get much simpler than this.

**Serves** / 4
**Prep** / 10 minutes  **Cook** / 1 hour 10 minutes  **Rest** / 15 minutes

6 chicken Marylands, cut through the joint to separate the drumsticks and thighs
¾ cup orange juice (about 1½ oranges, slice and reserve the leftover half)
Grated rind of 2 oranges
¼ cup honey
½ cup soy sauce
2 tbsp grated ginger
Salt, to season

Heat the oven to 190°C (fan-forced). Cut 2–3 deep slits into each drumstick, to the bone. Mix the remaining ingredients, except the salt, together in a large non-reactive bowl along with the chicken.

Place a few slices of orange on a lined baking tray, and arrange the drumstick portions of the chicken on top (making sure there is enough room for the thighs later), season with salt and bake for 20 minutes, basting with the marinade after 10 minutes. Add the thigh portions, season them with salt, and bake for a further 30 minutes, basting all the chicken pieces every 10 minutes until they are glossy, browned and cooked through.

Rest the chicken for 10 minutes before serving.

TIP / A tablespoon or two of Grand Marnier mixed through with the chicken before roasting adds a touch of sophistication to this uncomplicated dish.

# Orange baked chicken

This is a dish with a lot of history for me. I made it the first time I cooked for my family. I was eight years old, and I remember bursting with pride as I put it on the table and saw my whole family enjoying their meal. I think that was the exact moment I fell in love with cooking.

**Serves** / 6
**Prep** / 10 minutes  **Cook** / 50 minutes  **Rest** / 10 minutes

2 slices white bread, roughly torn
½ cup milk
2 tbsp vegetable oil
2 brown onions, peeled and
    roughly chopped
1kg beef mince
1 tsp salt
2 tbsp curry powder
2 tsp garam masala
1 Granny Smith apple, grated
1 tomato, halved and grated
    (skin discarded)
¼ cup mango or apricot chutney
    (or any fruit chutney) or 2 tbsp
    apricot jam
¼ cup dried sultanas
½ cup toasted almonds
6 bay leaves
Steamed rice and extra fruit chutney,
    to serve

**CUSTARD TOPPING**
2 eggs
1 cup milk
½ tsp turmeric

Heat the oven to 160°C (fan-forced). Soak the white bread in the milk for at least 10 minutes.

Meanwhile, heat the vegetable oil in a large baking dish or pot over high heat, fry the onions until softened then add the mince and continue to fry until browned. Stir through the salt, curry powder, garam masala, apple, tomato, chutney or jam, sultanas and almonds until well mixed. Add the milk-soaked bread and stir through the mince mixture. Scatter over the bay leaves, cover the dish or pot with foil or a lid and bake for 40 minutes.

For the custard topping, whisk together all the ingredients and set aside while the bobotie cooks.

Remove the bobotie from the oven, pour over the egg mixture and return to the hot oven on a grill setting for about 10 minutes, or until the custard is set and well browned. Serve the bobotie with rice and a little more fruit chutney on the side.

TIP / Grating tomatoes is an excellent way to extract the tomato flesh without needing to boil them to remove the skins. Just split a tomato completely in half horizontally and grate the cut side of the tomato against a box grater. The tomato flesh will be grated and the skin will flatten out so it can be thrown away easily.

# Bobotie

This delicious savoury mince dish with an egg custard topping is a classic of South African Cape Malay cuisine, and it's a dish with quite a history. Dutch trade routes around the southern parts of Africa brought influences from Indonesia, Malaysia, Sri Lanka and India and there are bobotie recipes that date back to the 17th century.

**Serves** / 6
**Prep** / 20 minutes  **Cook** / 1 hour

2 tbsp cumin seeds, or 2 tbsp
    ground cumin
6 cloves garlic, peeled
3 large red chillies
2 tbsp fish sauce
2 tbsp lime juice
1 tbsp vegetable oil
1 tbsp sugar
1 tsp salt flakes
1.5kg lamb forequarter chops
Coriander leaves, mint leaves and
    lime wedges, to serve

Toast the cumin seeds in a dry frypan and crush them to a very coarse powder with a mortar and pestle. There should still be a few large seeds remaining. Chop the garlic and chilli together on a chopping board until roughly chopped and well mixed. Mix the cumin and the garlic and chilli together with the fish sauce, lime juice, vegetable oil, sugar and salt and rub all over the lamb chops. Leave for 30 minutes to marinate.

Barbecue method: Grill the lamb chops on a very hot barbecue for about 4 minutes each side, or until well browned and cooked to your liking. Rest for about 5 minutes before serving.

Oven method: Heat the oven to 200°C (fan-forced). Arrange the lamb chops in a single layer on a foil-lined tray and bake, uncovered, for about 30 minutes, turning halfway through the cooking process.

Scatter the lamb with coriander and mint leaves and serve with lime wedges.

TIP / If you prefer a leaner cut, this same rub can be used for a lamb backstrap. Pan-fry or chargrill the marinated backstrap for about 3 minutes each side (or until cooked to your liking) and rest the meat for about 5 minutes before slicing and serving.

# Lamb chops with chilli, garlic & lime

I love Australian lamb. It stands up to strong flavours and remains moist and rich even when cooked for a long time. The toasty cumin in this recipe is enhanced by the heat of the chilli and contrasts well with the fresh coriander and mint. Ground cumin can be substituted for the toasted cumin seeds, but it will have a milder cumin flavour.

**Serves** / 6
**Prep** / 10 minutes  **Marinate** / 30 minutes  **Cook** / 10 minutes

6 large potatoes, freshly scrubbed

1 cup Otafuku sauce (see Tip)

2 sheets nori, thinly sliced

4 spring onions, trimmed and finely sliced

4 tbsp toasted sesame seeds, lightly crushed

A handful bonito flakes (optional)

Japanese mayonnaise, to serve

**PORK FILLING (OPTIONAL)**

1 tbsp vegetable oil

300g pork belly, roughly chopped, or pork mince

1 tbsp dark soy sauce

1 tbsp sake

½ tsp caster sugar

Heat the oven to 200°C. Wrap the potatoes individually in foil and bake for 60 minutes or until tender. Keep warm until ready to serve.

For the pork filling, heat the oil in a frypan over high heat and fry the pork until well browned. Add the soy sauce, sake and caster sugar and toss until the sugar is caramelised.

Split each potato in a cross nearly all the way through. Open the potato and fill the centre with pork and drizzle with Otafuku sauce. Scatter with the nori, spring onion, sesame seeds and bonito flakes (if using), and drizzle everything generously with mayonnaise.

TIP / Otafuku sauce is available from Japanese grocers. Alternatively you can make your own version by mixing together ½ cup tomato sauce, ¼ cup Worcestershire sauce, 2 tbsp soy sauce, 1 tbsp mirin, 1 tsp caster sugar and 1 tsp English mustard.

# Okonomipotato

One of my favourite Japanese foods is okonomiyaki, a kind of Japanese savoury pancake where the batter is mixed with whatever toppings take your fancy. But the toppings used with okonomiyaki are also fantastic in a baked potato. Try these with bacon and cheese, grilled prawns or any leftovers you may have in the fridge.

**Serves** / 6

**Prep** / 10 minutes  **Cook** / 1 hour 10 minutes

2 tbsp oil
500g beef mince
¼ cup soy sauce
1 tbsp caster sugar
1 can (400g) diced tomatoes
8 cups cooked short-grain rice, warm
3 avocados, peeled and thickly sliced
4 cups shredded cheese
½ head iceberg lettuce, shredded
1 red onion, peeled, halved and very
    thinly sliced
3 tomatoes, sliced

## TACO SEASONING
1 tbsp garlic powder, or 3 cloves garlic,
    peeled and crushed
2 tbsp ground cumin
1 tbsp ground paprika
1 tbsp chilli powder
2 tsp dried oregano
½ tsp black pepper
½ tsp salt

Heat the oil in a medium saucepan over high heat and brown the mince well. Add the taco seasoning ingredients (or use a commercial taco seasoning) and stir to coat. Add the soy sauce, sugar and tomatoes and bring to a simmer. Simmer for 20 minutes, stirring occasionally until the meat is cooked through.

Place the rice evenly on the bottom of a large baking dish and cover with the beef. Arrange the avocado slices over the beef and scatter everything with the shredded cheese. Grill under a very hot overhead grill for 5 minutes, or until the cheese is melted and browned.

Top the gratin with the lettuce, onion and tomato just before serving.

TIP / I love the taste of warm, buttery avocado when it is quickly grilled, but some varieties might become a little bitter if they are cooked for too long. If you prefer your avocado cold and fresh, just add it raw on top of the gratin with the lettuce, onion and tomato.

# Taco rice gratin

Taco rice is one of my favourite foods from Okinawa, a chain of islands forming the southernmost prefecture of Japan. Originally invented there by using surplus taco seasoning from US military provisions, it's now become a bit of an institution in the islands. This gratin version is perfect for feeding a family.

**Serves** / 6
**Prep** / 20 minutes  **Cook** / 35 minutes

1.2kg chicken thigh fillets, skinless
1 cup thick Greek-style yoghurt
3 tbsp Tandoori Paste (page 28)
Salt, to season
Cucumber Raita (page 227), to serve

Mix together the chicken, yoghurt and Tandoori Paste and massage it well into the chicken. Marinate covered in the fridge for at least 2 hours.

Oven method: Heat the oven to 240°C (fan-forced). Place the chicken in a single layer on a tray lined with baking paper or aluminium foil. Season with salt. Roast in the oven for 15 minutes. Turn off the oven but do not open the door, allowing the chicken to roast slowly for a further 10 minutes. Remove from the oven and rest for 10 minutes before serving.

Barbecue method: Season with salt. Grill the chicken on a very hot oiled grill for 3 minutes each side, or until just cooked through. Rest for 5 minutes before serving.

Serve the chicken with the Cucumber Raita.

**TIP** / This is a really easy dish to make, so make a double quantity and keep one portion aside to make Butter Chicken (page 129) later in the week.

# Tandoori chicken

Using a homemade paste can make all the difference with tandoori chicken. A very hot fan-forced oven is a good substitute for the intense heat of a true tandoor, but an oiled barbecue grill works well, too.

**Serves** / 6
**Prep** / 5 minutes  **Marinate** / 2 hours  **Cook** / 25 minutes  **Rest** / 10 minutes

- 1 whole snapper (about 1.5kg), gutted, cleaned and scaled
- 1 tbsp salt flakes
- 1 lime, thickly sliced
- 2 coriander roots, leaves picked and reserved, stems and roots roughly torn
- ½ cup Tom Yum Paste (page 23) or commercial paste
- ½ cup coconut cream
- ½ cup cherry or grape tomatoes, halved
- 1 cup loosely packed basil leaves, to serve
- Lime wedges, to serve

Heat the oven to 180°C (fan-forced). Line a baking tray with a double layer of foil large enough to totally encase the fish. Make deep cuts to the bone diagonally along both sides of the fish at 5cm intervals. Season the fish all over, inside and out with the salt flakes. Place the lime slices and torn coriander stems and roots in the cavity.

Mix together the Tom Yum Paste and coconut cream and spread it all over the fish, inside and out and underneath, and into the cuts. Wrap the fish completely in foil, firmly sealing the join of the foil at the top of the fish.

Bake the fish for 15 minutes, then open the foil, scrunching it around the fish so the whole of the fish is exposed but none of the juices leak out. Turn the oven to a hot grill setting and grill the fish for a further 8 minutes, or until the fish is toasted on top. Check that the fish is cooked – the flesh should pull away easily from the bone. If it is undercooked, grill for a few more minutes until it is cooked through.

Scatter with the reserved coriander leaves, tomato halves and basil leaves, and serve with lime wedges.

TIP / For a really impressive finish to this dish, deep-fry the basil leaves for a few seconds until they're crisp and scatter them over the fish to serve.

# Baked tom yum & coconut snapper

Cooking a whole fish is much easier than many might think. A well-cooked fish should be moist and come away easily from the bone. This simple method of baking whole fish is nearly foolproof, and the flavours of the tom yum paste and coconut are delicious with firm, white-fleshed fish such as snapper.

**Serves** / 4
**Prep** / 10 minutes  **Cook** / 25 minutes

# big
# sweets

2 cans (400ml each) coconut milk
30g powdered gelatin
1 can (400ml) evaporated milk
1 tsp coconut essence
1 cup caster sugar
3 egg whites

Pour one can of coconut milk into a large bowl, sprinkle over the gelatin and leave it to bloom for 5 minutes. Heat the remaining coconut milk, evaporated milk, coconut essence and caster sugar in a saucepan over medium heat until the sugar is dissolved, then whisk it through the gelatin mixture until all the crystals are completely dissolved. Place in the fridge for about 1 hour, or until the jelly has the consistency of thickened cream.

Whip the egg whites to stiff peaks and fold through the thick jelly. Transfer the jelly to a 20cm square cake tin lined with cling wrap and refrigerate for at least 4 hours until the jelly is set firm. Cut into 5cm cubes to serve.

**TIP** / Mayonnaises, mousses and any other foods made with raw egg should be stored in the fridge and are best eaten within 24 hours, both in terms of food safety and flavour.

# Coconut jelly

**Yeh jup goh** / This creamy Cantonese jelly is lightened with whipped egg whites to produce a delicate texture. It's one of my favourite sweets at yum cha, but unlike many of the things you see going around on the trolley, it's a cinch to make at home, too.

**Serves** / 8–10
**Prep** / 10 minutes **Cook** / 10 minutes **Refrigerate** / 5 hours

2 cups plain flour
1 cup rice flour
3 tbsp caster sugar
2 tbsp baking powder
3 eggs
½ can (200ml) evaporated milk
1 cup cold water
Vegetable oil or clarified butter,
    for greasing the pan
50g salted butter
2 cups crushed roasted peanuts
1 cup soft brown sugar
Good-quality chocolate ice cream,
    to serve

Mix the dry ingredients together in a large bowl and whisk the eggs, evaporated milk and water in a separate bowl. Whisk the liquids into the solids a little at a time and fold gently to a smooth batter. Strain the batter through a fine sieve and stand in the fridge for at least 1 hour before cooking.

Heat a 20cm frypan over medium heat and grease with a little paper towel soaked in oil. Add a large ladle of batter to the pan and spread it over the base and a little up the sides of the pan. Cook the pancake until dry on top and crisp underneath.

Rub the top of the pancake with a little butter and scatter generously with peanuts and brown sugar. Fold the pancake over and serve with a scoop of ice cream.

**TIP** / In Malaysia these are often filled with spoonfuls of creamed corn along with the peanuts. If that's a bit too adventurous for you but you want to try a variation on this, scatter some good quality chocolate chips and/or sliced banana among the peanuts.

# Peanut pancakes

**Apam balik** / These folded peanut pancakes are a hugely popular market snack in Malaysia. In the heat of the Malaysian outdoors they are enjoyed as is, but the best thing about making them at home is you get to team them with chocolate ice cream. It's like they were made for each other.

**Serves** / 6
**Prep** / 15 minutes  **Refrigerate** / 1 hour  **Cook** / 20 minutes

## CREAM CHEESE CUSTARD

1 cup milk
250g cream cheese
6 egg yolks
25g caster sugar
60g plain flour
15g cornflour
2 tbsp lemon juice

## MERINGUE

6 egg whites
100g caster sugar

## HONEY GLAZE

1 tbsp honey
1 tbsp soft brown sugar
1 tbsp unsalted butter, plus extra
for brushing

Heat the oven to 180°C. Line a 22cm square baking tin with baking paper and brush the paper with a little melted butter.

To make the cream cheese custard, place the milk and cream cheese in a small saucepan over medium heat, whisking occasionally until the mixture is smooth. In a separate heatproof bowl, whisk the egg yolks and caster sugar together until the sugar is dissolved then add the cream cheese mixture, pouring in a thin stream, whisking continuously to combine. Sift in the flour and cornflour and whisk to form a smooth custard. Stir through the lemon juice and set aside.

To make the meringue, whisk the egg whites to soft peaks then gradually add the caster sugar, whisking constantly until the meringue is firm and glossy. A stand mixer is perfect for this. Whisk a third of the meringue into the cream cheese custard, then gently fold through the remainder of the meringue until the mixture is well combined.

Pour the cheesecake mixture into the tin and smooth the top. Place the tin in a tall-sided baking tray and pour hot water around the cake tin until it reaches about 2cm up the side of the tin.

Place the cake in the oven and immediately turn the heat down to 160°C. Bake for 1 hour, but check the cake after 50 minutes and if the top has not browned, increase the oven temperature to 180°C for the final ten minutes of cooking. Turn off the oven and wedge a wooden spoon into the door to keep it open a crack.

Allow the cheesecake to cool in the oven for 45 minutes then remove. The cheesecake should have shrunk back away from the sides of the tin and reduced in height evenly, without sinking in the middle.

For the glaze, combine the honey, brown sugar and butter and melt the mixture in a small saucepan or by heating in the microwave for about 20 seconds. Brush the top of the cake generously with the glaze.

Allow the cake to cool to room temperature, then refrigerate overnight in an airtight container. Slice and serve.

TIP / Don't use a removable-base tin for this cheesecake. It isn't necessary and it can allow the bain-marie water to seep into the cake, leaving you with a soggy base.

# Japanese soufflé cheesecake

This fluffy, soufflé-style baked cheesecake is hugely popular in Japan for its moist and smooth texture that is far lighter than many baked cheesecakes. Refrigerating the cake overnight will improve its texture and enhance its creamy flavour.

**Serves** / 8
**Prep** / 25 minutes  **Cook** / 1 hour  **Cool** / 45 minutes  **Refrigerate** / overnight

600ml water
150g palm sugar, roughly chopped
6 bananas, peeled and cut into large, irregular pieces
1 can (400ml) coconut milk
2 pandan leaves, tied in a knot, or 1 tsp vanilla extract (optional)
A good pinch of salt

Bring the water and palm sugar to the boil in a large saucepan, stirring to ensure the sugar is completely dissolved. Add the bananas, coconut milk, pandan leaves or vanilla (if using), and salt. Stir gently and bring to the boil. As soon as the coconut milk boils, remove from the heat.

You can either serve warm, at room temperature or chilled with cubes of ice floating on top for a refreshing summer dessert.

TIP / Pandan leaves are available both fresh and frozen from Asian grocers. If you like you can add ¼ cup of dry sago pearls at the same time as the bananas and coconut milk and simmer for about 10 minutes until the pearls are translucent, then allow the mixture to stand covered for a further 10 minutes before serving.

# Bananas in coconut milk

**Pengat pisang** / It doesn't get much simpler than this. With a tin of coconut milk, a block of palm sugar in the pantry and bananas in the fruit bowl, you'll never be without a special dessert for an Asian meal. Vanilla is a great substitute for pandan, as they have a similar toasty, umami flavour.

**Serves** / 6
**Prep** / 10 minutes **Cook** / 15 minutes

Vegetable oil, for deep frying,
    plus 1 tbsp additional oil
3 Granny Smith apples, peeled
    and cut into bite-sized cubes
2 cups caster sugar
1 cup water
2 tbsp toasted sesame seeds

**BATTER**
1 cup plain flour
¼ cup cornflour
¾ cup cold water

For the batter, mix together the flour and cornflour and add the cold water, mixing just enough to create a thin batter. Don't mix it too much – a few lumps is fine.

Heat the oil in a wok, large saucepan or deep-fryer to 180°C. Toss the apples through the batter and deep-fry in batches for 3 minutes, or until golden brown. Drain on paper towel and keep warm in the oven until ready to serve.

In a large saucepan or wok add 1 tbsp of fresh vegetable oil, caster sugar and water and bring to the boil. Swirl the pan to ensure the sugar is dissolved and no crystals appear on the edges of the pot. Boil the sugar syrup, uncovered, for about 10 minutes, or until a golden toffee is formed. Add all the warm fried apples to the saucepan at once, and toss to completely coat in the toffee.

Tip the toffee apples out onto a warmed plate and scatter with sesame seeds. Serve immediately with bowls of iced water. Take a little apple from the plate, dip it into the water to harden the toffee, and eat it straight away.

**TIP** / You can make these without the batter for a lighter dessert. Don't worry about scrubbing the plates or pots clean after the toffee has hardened, just leave them sitting in warm water for a while and the toffee will dissolve easily.

# Chinese toffee apples

My mother lives near a small village just outside Beijing and whenever I visit we eat at our favourite local restaurant. One of my favourite desserts is a big plate of toffee apples. Fritters of apple are tossed in warm toffee and brought straight to the table with bowls of iced water. We grab chunks with our chopsticks and dip them into the water to harden the toffee.

**Serves** / 6
**Prep** / 20 minutes  **Cook** / 15 minutes

75g caster sugar
¼ tsp salt
1 tsp baking powder
2 cups plain flour
200g unsalted butter, softened
2 eggs, plus an additional egg yolk,
    beaten, for brushing
1 cup blanched almonds

Heat the oven to 160°C. Mix together the sugar, salt, baking powder and flour in a large bowl and rub in the butter until the mixture resembles breadcrumbs. Mix through the 2 eggs, just until the batter comes together into a soft dough. Cover with cling wrap and refrigerate for at least 30 minutes.

Roll the dough into a long sausage about 2cm in diameter, then cut into rounds at 2cm intervals. Place the rounds on a lined baking sheet standing on their cut end and press down with the heel of your palm to flatten. Press a blanched almond (or almond half) into the centre of each cookie. Brush the tops of the cookies with beaten egg yolk.

Bake the cookies for 20 minutes, or until lightly browned and glossy. Allow to cool on the tray, and serve.

**TIP /** The basic butter cookie dough and method can be used for many other variations of butter cookies. Try mixing through chocolate chips or lemon rind, or just roll the dough out into a thin sheet and cut shapes with cookie cutters.

# Almond butter cookies

Years ago when I worked in a Chinese restaurant one of my first tasks each day was to make crumbly almond cookies that were served with coffee. There was nothing better than eating them fresh out of the oven. The chefs would measure out ingredients with the old Chinese balance scales measuring catties and taels. Luckily, this version is a bit easier to follow.

**Makes** / About 60 cookies
**Prep** / 25 minutes  **Refrigerate** / 30 minutes  **Cook** / 20 minutes

1 cup milk

A large pinch of saffron steeped in 2 tbsp hot water

1 can (375ml) evaporated milk

1 can (395g or 300ml) sweetened condensed milk

300ml thickened cream

2 cups fresh mango pulp (blended from the flesh of 2–3 large mangoes)

1 cup shelled pistachios, lightly crushed, to serve

Place the milk, saffron and its steeping water in a small saucepan, bring to the boil and remove from the heat. Watch this carefully as it can easily boil over.

In a large bowl, combine the evaporated milk, condensed milk and cream then pour over the hot milk and saffron and whisk everything together. Whisk in the mango pulp and place the bowl in the freezer for two hours, or until softly set. Whisk firmly to break up any ice crystals.

Line a 2-litre capacity loaf or terrine tin with cling wrap (leave some hanging over the edges) and pour in the kulfi, pressing it into the corners if necessary. Make sure the top is smooth and flat. Freeze for a further 2 hours, or until firmly set.

Turn out the kulfi and scatter with pistachios. Cut thick slices to serve.

TIP / To make the mango pulp, remove the flesh from the mangoes and process for a few seconds in a food processor, or finely chop it on a cutting board. Reserve any juices and recombine them with the pulp.

# Mango kulfi with pistachios

Kulfi is the rich, thick Indian answer to ice cream, but the best thing about it is you don't need an ice cream machine to make it. A slice of this mango kulfi with a touch of saffron is the perfect finish to an Indian meal.

**Serves** / 6–8
**Prep** / 10 minutes **Cook** / 10 minutes **Freeze** / 4 hours

1 litre water
25g powdered gelatin
½ cup instant coffee powder
1 cup caster sugar
300ml thickened cream

Add about a cup of the water (250ml) to the powdered gelatin in a small bowl and allow it to stand for about 10 minutes. Bring the remaining 750ml of water to a low simmer then add the coffee and sugar, whisking to dissolve the sugar.

Add the gelatin mix to the coffee liquid and whisk well to ensure all the gelatin crystals are dissolved (you may need to rinse the gelatin bowl with the hot coffee liquid a few times to remove any crystals still clinging to the bowl).

Pour the coffee liquid into a 20cm × 30cm shallow cake tin to a depth of about 2cm. Refrigerate for 4 hours, or until the jelly is well set.

Cut the jelly into 2cm cubes and serve with a few spoonfuls of thickened cream.

TIP / Use decaffeinated coffee if you're sensitive to caffeine. The jelly can also be set in individual glasses and topped with cream or vanilla ice cream and a sprinkling of cocoa.

# Coffee jelly

This is a fantastic dessert for feeding a crowd. It's simple and economical to make, light to eat, keeps well, and you don't need a lot of it for a satisfyingly sweet end to a meal. You might even find yourself tucking into it the next morning for 'breakfast dessert'!

**Serves** / 6–8
**Prep** / 15 minutes  **Cook** / 5 minutes  **Refrigerate** / 4 hours

½ seedless watermelon
Lemon wedges, to garnish

**GRANITA SYRUP**
½ cup water
½ cup caster sugar
1 cinnamon stick
2 tbsp lemon juice

To make the granita syrup, bring the water, sugar and cinnamon to a simmer, stirring to dissolve the sugar. Allow to cool, then remove the cinnamon stick and stir through the lemon juice.

Place a metal tray in the freezer. Cut the half-watermelon in half again and scoop the flesh from one side. Cover the remaining side with cling wrap and keep in the fridge until ready to serve. Blend the flesh in a food processor or blender and strain the juice through a fine sieve, discarding any pulp. Stir the watermelon juice through the granita syrup and chill in the fridge for 30 minutes. Transfer to the tray in the freezer and freeze for about 5 hours, scraping the granita with a fork every couple of hours until well frozen, fluffy and flaky.

When the granita is frozen, place a large serving platter in the freezer until it is very cold. Remove the remaining watermelon from the fridge, slice it into wedges and arrange on the platter with a few lemon wedges. Scrape the granita one final time and spoon it all over the cold watermelon. Serve immediately.

**TIP** / This is also a perfect dish for a summer barbecue. Chilling the plate and watermelon before adding the granita will stop it from melting too quickly. It doesn't really matter though, as it will be all gone before the granita has a chance to melt anyway!

# Watermelon
# & watermelon

A platter of fresh fruit is a classic end to a Chinese meal, but it doesn't have to be boring. Adding a watermelon granita to a platter of cold watermelon is a great way to turn a simple fruit platter into something truly memorable. The hint of cinnamon in the granita adds warmth to the watermelon's natural freshness.

**Serves** / 10–12
**Prep** / 20 minutes  **Cook** / 5 minutes  **Freeze** / 5½ hours

1 medium Kent or other Japanese
  pumpkin (as close to 2½kg
  as possible)
5 eggs
200ml thick coconut cream, scooped
  from the top of an unshaken can
¼ cup grated palm sugar
½ cup caster sugar

Heat the oven to 180°C. Holding a small, sharp knife at an angle, carefully cut a large 'lid' around the stalk of the pumpkin and remove it. With a strong spoon or melon baller, scoop all the seeds and membrane from the centre of the pumpkin.

Beat the eggs until smooth and add the coconut cream and sugars, whisking constantly. Pour the custard mix through a sieve into the centre of the pumpkin, filling up to the inside edge of the hole where the 'lid' was removed.

Place the pumpkin in a large round cake tin just big enough to fit it, and place the cake tin on a larger baking tray. Bake the pumpkin for 2½ hours, checking its firmness by tapping the side of the pumpkin and watching for the wobble in the top of the custard. If you like, you can bake the 'lid' separately, removing it from the oven after about 45 minutes, or when it is cooked through. When the custard begins to firm, turn off the oven and leave the pumpkin inside to cool for a further 2 hours or overnight. Slice and serve.

TIP / The size of the pumpkin is very important to the cooking time for this dish, as is the thickness of the coconut cream. Don't shake the can of coconut cream before opening, and use a spoon to scoop the thickest cream plug that has risen to the top of the can. Discard the watery portion at the bottom of the can, or use it in dishes such as the Big Red Curry (page 100).

# Pumpkin custard

**Sankaya** / You'd never guess that something that looks this dramatic was so simple to prepare. The coconut egg custard matches really well with the melony sweetness of the pumpkin. In Thai cuisine it's usually steamed in a huge steamer, but this baked version is much easier.

**Serves** / 8
**Prep** / 15 minutes  **Cook** / 2½ hours  **Rest** / 2 hours

## CARAMEL

1½ cups caster sugar

## MERINGUE

8 egg whites
1 tsp cream of tartar
½ cup caster sugar

## ORANGE CUSTARD

4 egg yolks
¼ cup caster sugar
¼ cup orange liqueur such as
    Grand Marnier or Cointreau
1 can (400ml) evaporated milk

2 mangoes, sliced, to serve

For the caramel, heat the caster sugar in a small saucepan until a dark caramel is formed. Pour the caramel around the edges of a 2-litre bundt tin and rotate the tin, ensuring it is completely covered.

Heat the oven to 180°C. To make the meringue, whip the egg whites to soft peaks then add the cream of tartar and sugar gradually while whisking to firm peaks. Fill the bundt tin with the meringue mixture and flatten the top. Place the bundt tin inside a tall-sided baking tray and pour hot water around the tin until it reaches about 2cm up the side of the tin. Bake for 30 minutes, or until browned on top. Remove from the oven and allow to cool in the tin for about 30 minutes. Invert the tin to place the meringue on a serving platter.

While the meringue is cooking, to make the orange custard whisk the egg yolks, caster sugar and liqueur together in a heatproof bowl. Heat the evaporated milk in a small saucepan until steaming and pour over the egg mixture, stirring constantly with a wooden spoon. Return the milk and egg mix to the saucepan and stir over low heat for about 15 minutes, or until the custard thickens. Serve the canonigo with the warm custard and fresh mango slices.

TIP / Try not to incorporate air into the custard while it cooks, so use a wooden spoon and not a whisk. Air bubbles may create a foam, which will spoil the custard.

# Canonigo

This Filipino dessert is part île flottante, part crème caramel and part pavlova. Combining these could never be a bad thing, and although it may seem complicated, it's actually much easier to make than any of them individually. I love the combination of the orange custard and fresh mango, and of course a caramel-coated meringue is the stuff dreams are made of.

**Serves** / 6
**Prep** / 30 minutes   **Cook** / 30 minutes   **Cool** / 30 minutes

# little
# sides

¼ cup dark soy sauce
1 tsp caster sugar
3 cups water
1 star anise
2 cinnamon sticks
½ onion, peeled and roughly chopped
4 dried shiitake mushrooms, quickly rinsed
4 tea bags Lady Grey tea, or other black tea
8 Steamed Eggs (page 228) (steamed for 8 minutes)

Mix together all the ingredients except the eggs in a non-reactive saucepan, cover and bring the mixture to the boil. Remove from the heat and allow to cool to room temperature without removing the lid. Remove the tea bags.

Carefully crack the shell of the eggs all over, making sure there are lots of small cracks but the shell remains around the egg. Add the eggs to the tea mixture. Allow the eggs to steep for at least 5 hours, then remove from the liquid. Peel and eat.

TIP / Although in many Asian cultures flavoured eggs are cooked for a long time until they are firm and pungent, I prefer them lightly cooked and soft inside, so I steep the eggs in room-temperature liquid rather than hot. It takes longer and the eggs take up less marbling, but you can control the texture of the egg more easily. Use these eggs in a dish of Udon with Friends (page 34), or to accompany some Hakka Noodles (page 120) or Chicken, Mushrooms and Snow Peas (page 74).

# Tea eggs

Tea eggs are a beautiful and simple Chinese snack or accompaniment. Any black tea can be used, but I prefer Lady Grey. The light citrus hints of lemon, orange and bergamot are a great substitute for the dried tangerine more commonly used in this recipe.

**Serves** / 8
**Prep** / 10 minutes  **Cook** / 10 minutes
**Steep** / 5 hours

½ head cabbage
1 tsp salt
2 tbsp sugar
½ cup white vinegar
1 cup water
3 dried chillies, finely sliced
1 tsp Sichuan peppercorns (optional)

Tear or slice the cabbage into large chunks about 5cm square. Place in a non-reactive bowl and scatter over the salt. Toss well to coat, place a plate on top and weigh it down (an unopened can works well as a weight). Allow to stand at room temperature for 2 hours.

In a non-reactive saucepan heat the sugar, vinegar and water to a low simmer, stirring to dissolve the sugar. Remove from the heat and add the chillies and Sichuan peppercorns (if using). Allow to cool. Pour the pickling liquid over the cabbage (do not drain the cabbage first). Stir well, replace the weight and refrigerate for at least 1 hour before serving. The pickle will keep for about two weeks in the fridge.

TIP / I love the contrast between this crunchy cabbage pickle and soft white rice served with Chinese dishes. Try this as an accompaniment to some Drunken Chicken (page 130), Grandma's Tofu (page 69), or Pork and Eggplant (page 85).

# Pickled cabbage

A traditional Sichuan pickle is made by fermenting and souring cabbage in a brine solution containing white rice spirit for a week or so. This simple version with vinegar is faster, easier and just as tasty.

**Makes** / 2 cups
**Prep** / 5 minutes  **Cook** / 5 minutes
**Stand** / 3 hours

3 Lebanese cucumbers, peeled at intervals
1 tsp salt
5cm ginger, peeled and sliced into very thin matchsticks

Slice the cucumbers on a steep diagonal into 5mm slices. Place in a press-seal bag and scatter with the salt and ginger. Massage for a minute to mix the salt, then squeeze as much air as possible out of the bag and seal firmly. Allow to stand in the fridge for 3 hours. When ready, the cucumber should be slightly softened and swimming in released liquid.

TIP / A small serve of these pickles on the side will improve just about any Asian meal, but try this with some Snapper Rice (page 96), Drunken Chicken (page 130) or Teriyaki Steak (page 135).

# Ginger-pickled cucumber

Pickles are vital to many Asian cuisines. In Japan, a bowl of rice, miso soup and an assortment of pickles is a perfectly acceptable meal. This cucumber pickle is so simple it really is worth having some in your fridge all the time.

**Makes** / 3 cups
**Prep** / 10 minutes  **Stand** / 3 hours

2 cups small red radishes, cleaned and quartered
   (leave a little green stem on if you can)
1 tsp salt
2 tbsp caster sugar
2 tbsp rice vinegar

Place all the ingredients in a press-seal bag and massage for a few minutes until the radishes start to release their liquid. Squeeze as much air out of the bag as possible and seal firmly. Place the bag in the fridge overnight, but the pickles will be better after a few days.

TIP / This is a Japanese-style pickle and as such it works well with many Japanese dishes. Try this with Snapper Rice (page 96), Barbecue Noodles (page 147) or Steak and Asparagus Donburi (page 156).

# Red radish pickles

A simple radish pickle is a great accompaniment to many dishes. A good whack of sugar offsets the sharp bitterness of the radish, and the resulting fresh flavour is a great way to lighten oily savoury dishes.

**Makes** / About 2 cups
**Prep** / 5 minutes  **Refrigerate** / Overnight

¼ large Japanese pumpkin, peeled and cut into chunks
1–2 spring onions, trimmed and sliced
¼ cup Japanese mayonnaise
Salt and freshly ground black pepper, to season
¼ cup toasted almonds, lightly crushed

Place the pumpkin chunks in a medium saucepan and cover with cold water. Bring the water to a simmer and simmer the pumpkin for about 8 minutes. Drain well and allow to cool.

Roughly mash the pumpkin, leaving some large chunks. Stir through the spring onions and mayonnaise, and season well with salt and pepper.

Scatter with well-toasted almonds before serving, chilled or at room temperature.

TIP / Try serving this as a side dish to some Nori Butter Roast Chicken (page 179), Nikujaga (page 104), or even some Lamb Kheema Curry (page 116).

4 cups Cabbage Dashi (page 17)
2 cups baby spinach
150g silken tofu, drained and cut into 2cm cubes
3 tbsp miso paste, any kind
2 spring onions, trimmed and finely sliced

Bring the Cabbage Dashi to a simmer in a medium saucepan. Add the spinach and tofu and stir over medium heat for a minute or two, or until the spinach is wilted. Remove from the heat.

Place the miso in a fine sieve, dip the sieve into the soup and with the back of a ladle dissolve it into the liquid. Discard any undissolved soy bean or rice pieces left in the sieve.

Place a teaspoon of spring onion slices in the bottom of a small bowl, ladle over the hot soup and serve immediately.

TIP / This recipe can be scaled to suit any number of people. Just remember the basics: about ¾ tbsp of miso per cup of liquid (less if your stock is already salted), and never boil the soup after adding the miso.

# Japanese pumpkin salad

This simple Japanese-style pumpkin salad is a great alternative to potato salad. The natural sweetness of the pumpkin combined with the toasty crunch of the almonds is a truly excellent combination.

# Basic miso soup

This is an almost universal Japanese side dish. The secret is never to bring the soup to the boil after adding the miso, as boiling spoils its texture. Although wakame (green seaweed) is commonly used in miso soup, it can be made with any leafy green vegetable. Here I've used spinach.

**Makes** / About 2 cups
**Prep** / 10 minutes  **Cook** / 10 minutes

**Serves** / 4
**Prep** / 5 minutes  **Cook** / 5 minutes

2 Lebanese cucumbers, unpeeled
½ tsp salt
2 cups Greek-style yoghurt
A handful mint leaves, finely shredded
¼ tsp ground cumin

Remove the ends of the cucumbers and split them in half lengthways. Scrape out the seeds with a teaspoon and discard.

Grate the cucumbers into a bowl and scatter with the salt. Transfer to a fine sieve and allow the cucumbers to drain for 10 minutes. Squeeze out any excess liquid by gently pressing the grated cucumber against the sieve.

Mix the drained cucumber with the yoghurt, mint and cumin and serve.

TIP / You can make this raita with carrot, onion or even pineapple. For a thicker texture, first hang the yoghurt in cheesecloth or a clean tea towel to extract some of its liquid. Try this with some Lamb Vindaloo (page 107), Tandoori Chicken (page 191) or even with Lamb Chops with Chilli, Garlic and Lime (page 184).

# Cucumber raita

This lovely cooling raita is perfect for combating the heat of spicy curries, but you don't need to limit it just to Indian dishes. It's also great with lamb chops, grilled fish and roasted vegetables.

**Makes** / About 2½ cups
**Prep** / 15 minutes

2 ripe tomatoes, at room temperature, sliced into rounds
½ red onion, peeled and very thinly sliced into rings
Salt flakes and freshly ground black pepper, to season

**DRESSING**
1 tbsp rice vinegar
½ tsp caster sugar
1 tsp soy sauce
1 tsp sesame oil

Place the tomatoes on a chilled plate and pile the onions on top. Season well with salt and pepper. Mix together the dressing ingredients and pour over the salad. Serve immediately.

TIP / Never keep your tomatoes in the fridge, it spoils their flavour. If you like tomatoes cold, dip them in iced water for about a minute immediately before slicing and eating. This salad is a perfect match with Teriyaki Steak (page 135), Tiger-skin Chicken (page 165) or Nori Butter Roast Chicken (page 179).

# Tomato salad

This simple salad is an ideal fresh accompaniment to many Japanese dishes, but it also works well with Indian food.

**Serves** / As a side dish
**Prep** / 5 minutes

2 Lebanese cucumbers, peeled in intervals, halved and sliced

2 large red shallots, peeled and thinly sliced

2 large red chillies, cut into irregular chunks

**VINEGAR SYRUP**

½ cup white vinegar

½ cup caster sugar

½ cup water

To make the vinegar syrup, place the ingredients in a saucepan and bring to a simmer, stirring until the sugar is dissolved. Allow to cool to room temperature.

Combine the vegetables in a bowl, pour over the cooled syrup and serve immediately at room temperature. If you want to refrigerate this for use later, it will become a slightly more conventional pickle.

TIP / This is the perfect side dish to go with Baked Thai Fish Cakes (page 172), Kuku Paka (page 91), or Thai-style Braised Pork (page 99).

As many eggs as you like

Bring plenty of water to the boil in a steamer and when steaming strongly add as many eggs as you like to the steamer basket. Steam, covered, for 6 minutes for soft yolks and gelatinous whites, 8 minutes for bright, buttery yolks and silky whites, and 10 minutes for firm yolks and tender, springy whites.

Remove the eggs from the steamer and place in a bowl of tap water to cool. Peel as soon as the eggs are cool enough to handle.

TIP / To peel the eggs cleanly, break off a little of the shell just after adding them to the water to cool, making sure you also break the membrane just inside the shell. As the egg cools a tiny amount of water will be sucked into the egg and push the white away from the shell. For the same reason, it can also help to peel eggs under running water. Once you have your Steamed Eggs try making some Tea Eggs (page 220), or add them to the Hokkaido Soup Curry (page 119), Thai-style Braised Pork (page 99), or Soy Sauce Chicken (page 126).

# Ajat

This excellent condiment is part dressing, part chutney and part pickle. A simple vinegar syrup is poured over fresh cucumber, shallot and chilli and served immediately. The result is a sweet and sour accompaniment that can be added to a huge number of main dishes for a cleansing hit of acidity, sweetness and crisp texture.

**Makes** / 2 cups
**Prep** / 10 minutes  **Cook** / 5 minutes

# Steamed eggs

If anyone tells me they can't even boil an egg, my usual reply is that I haven't boiled an egg for years myself. Steamed eggs are tastier, cleaner and easier to make than the boiled ones. The gentle heat of steaming keeps the whites tender and silky, and the texture of the yolk can be controlled to the finest degree.

**Serves** / Per egg
**Cook** / 6–10 minutes

'I hope somewhere in this book there is a dish or two that you choose to serve to your family. Something that gets asked for again and again, and each time you make it, it becomes a little more your own. Then one day, years from now, when the people you cook for have left and live their lives and come back to visit, you make that meal for them again. And that's what makes them feel like they're home.'

# Index

# Index

# Index

One of the best things about writing a cookbook in the digital age is seeing the dishes brought to life in people's homes. Let me know how you went with the recipes, or upload a photo of something you've cooked from this book or my other cookbooks, *Asian After Work* or *Two Asian Kitchens*. Perhaps you have some suggestions of what you might want to see in future books, or even if you just want to say hello, you can contact me through my website, or on Facebook, Instagram, Twitter or Youtube. I'd love to hear from you.

www.adamliaw.com
www.facebook.com/AdamLiawFanPage
www.instagram.com/liawadam
www.twitter.com/adamliaw
www.youtube.com/adamliaw

Published in Australia and New Zealand in 2014
by Hachette Australia
(an imprint of Hachette Australia Pty Limited)
Level 17, 207 Kent Street, Sydney NSW 2000
www.hachette.com.au

10 9 8 7 6 5 4 3 2 1

National Library of Australia
Cataloguing-in-Publication data:

Liaw, Adam, author.

Adam's big pot / Adam Liaw.

978 0 7336 3069 9 (paperback)

One-dish meals.

641.82

Photography by Steve Brown
Art direction by Reuben Crossman
Food styling by Jenn Tolhurst
Food preparation by Olivia Andrews
Typeset in Domaine Display and Calibre by Klim
Printed in China by 1010 Printing International

With special thanks to Alison Fraser from 'Slab and Slub' for her beautiful handmade ceramics and textiles. Please contact her at slabandslub.com.au or alison@slabandslub.com.au

Thanks to Le Creuset Australia www.lecreuset.com.au